Famous Art Heists

Sally Cowan

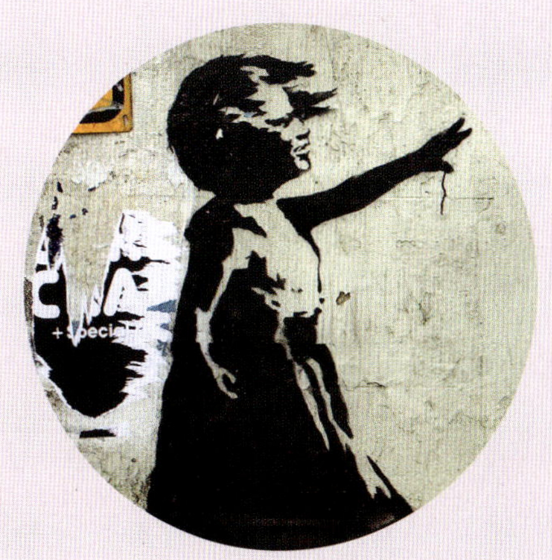

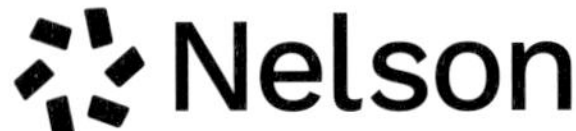

Famous Art Heists

Text: Sally Cowan
Publishers: Tania Mazzeo and Eliza Webb
Series consultant: Amanda Sutera
Hands on Heads Consulting
Editor: Kirstie Innes-Will
Project editors: Annabel Smith
Designer: Leigh Ashforth
Project designer: Danielle Maccarone
Permissions researchers: Lumina Datamatics
Production controller: Renee Tome

Acknowledgements
We would like to thank the following for permission to reproduce copyright material:

Front cover: powerofforever/E+/Getty Images p. 4, back cover: Pixel-Shot/Shutterstock.com; p. 5: UPI/Alamy Stock Photo; p. 6: Universal History Archive/Universal Images Group/Getty Images; p. 7: (top) North Wind Picture Archives/Alamy Stock Photo; (bottom) Science History Images/Alamy Stock Photo; p. 8: (top) Sueddeutsche Zeitung Photo/Alamy Stock Photo; (bottom) Roger Viollet/Getty Images; p. 9: (top) Heritage Image Partnership Ltd/Alamy Stock Photo; (bottom); p. 10: ullstein bild/ullstein bild/Getty Images; p. 11: Philip Game/Alamy Stock Photo; p. 12: (top) Smith Archive/Alamy Stock Photo; (bottom): Bruce Postle/Nine Entertainment Company; p. 13: FAIRFAX MEDIA/Nine Entertainment Company; p.14: Philip Game/Alamy Stock Photo; p. 15: Bill Waterson/Alamy Stock Photo; p. 16: (top) Pictorial Press Ltd/Alamy Stock Photo; (bottom) POLICE/AFP/Getty Images; p. 17: (top) -/AFP/Getty Images; (bottom) Universal History Archive/Universal Images Group/Getty Images; p. 18: (top) Trinity Mirror/Alamy Stock Photo; p. 19: Johnny Greig/Alamy Stock Photo; p. 20: Hemis/Alamy Stock Photo; p. 21: (top) picture alliance/picture alliance/Getty Images; (bottom), (title page) Barry Lewis/Alamy Stock Photo; p. 22: Jack Taylor/Getty Images News/Getty Images; p. 23: (top) DCOW/Alamy Stock Photo; (bottom) imageBROKER.com GmbH & Co. KG/Alamy Stock Photo; p. 24: (top) Triff/Shutterstock.com; (bottom) Ashley Cooper/Alamy Stock Photo; p. 25: AFP/DDP/Getty Images; p. 26: picture alliance/picture alliance/Getty Images; p. 27: (top) dpa picture alliance/Alamy Stock Photo; (bottom) picture alliance/picture alliance/Getty Images; p. 28: dpa picture alliance/Alamy Stock Photo; p. 29: Diego Grandi/Shutterstock.com; p. 30: Christopher Furlong/Getty Images Entertainment/Getty Images.

NovaStar

ISBN 978 0 17 033521 8

Cengage Learning Australia
Level 5, 80 Dorcas Street
Southbank VIC 3006 Australia
Phone: 1300 790 853
Email: aust.nelsonprimary@cengage.com

For learning solutions, visit **cengage.com.au**

Printed in China by 1010 Printing International Ltd
1 2 3 4 5 6 7 29 28 27 26 25

Nelson acknowledges the Traditional Owners and Custodians of the lands of all First Nations Peoples. We pay respect to Elders past and present, and extend that respect to all First Nations Peoples today.

Contents

What Is a Heist?

In art galleries and museums all around the world, there are valuable artworks such as paintings, sculptures and jewellery on display for people to enjoy. In the past, some of these artworks have been stolen by thieves. Usually, there are strict security measures in place at galleries and museums to prevent robberies. But when they do occur, these kinds of robberies seem so well-planned and **audacious** that they are given a special name: "**heist**" (pronounced *hye-st*).

There have been some famous heists in the last hundred years or so. They have shocked and distressed the public, because the stolen items were of **cultural** importance. Some of the thieves took advantage of lapses in security to grab artworks, while others planned the heist carefully.

Art galleries usually have security cameras, making it hard to pull off a heist.

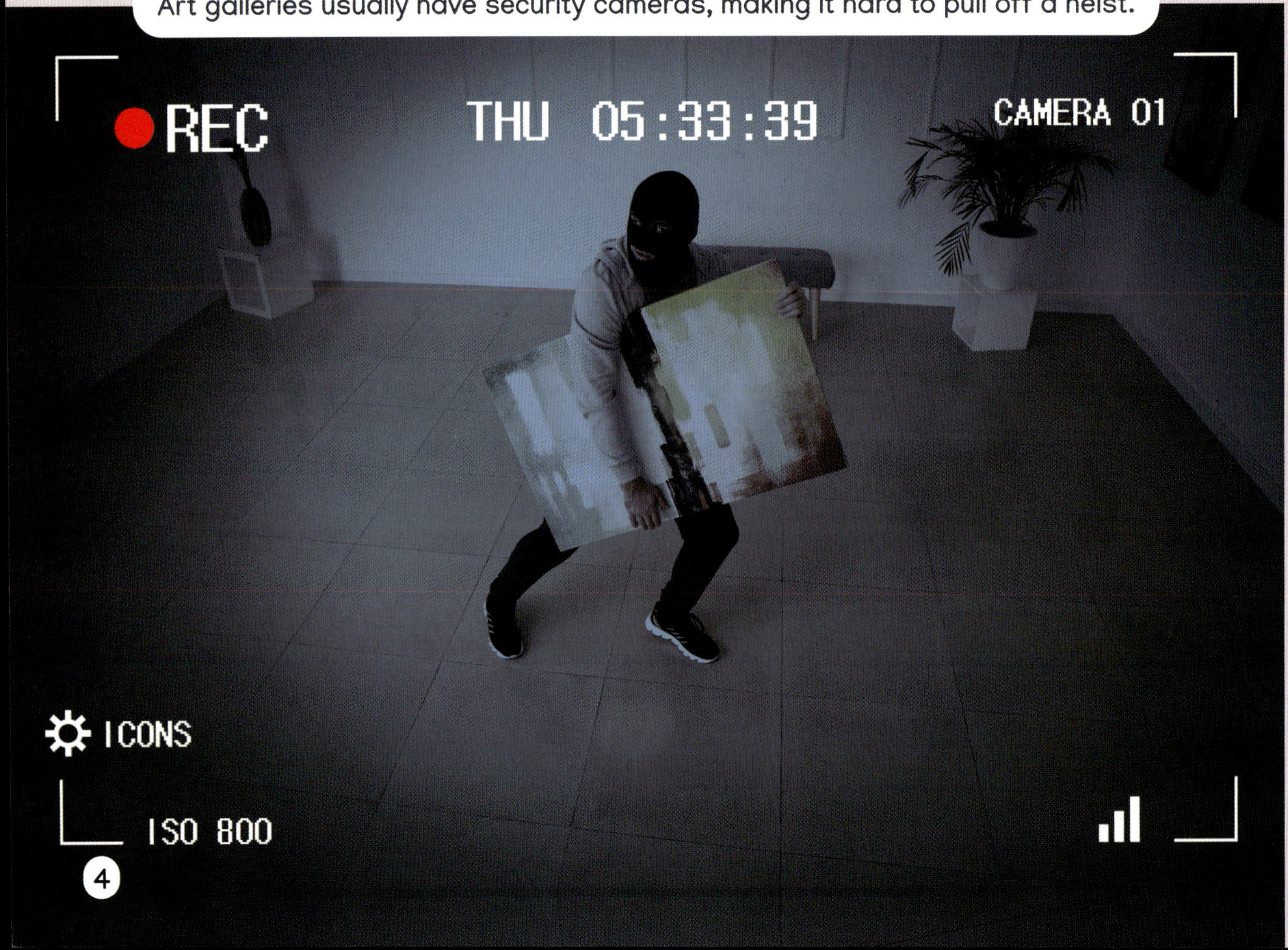

The thieves had different **motives** for carrying out their heists. Mostly, they wanted to get rich! But there were other reasons, too. One famous heist was meant to be a **patriotic** act of returning a **masterpiece** to its country of origin. Another heist was done to draw attention to the lack of funding for the arts in a large city, and yet another may have been to distract police from investigating the thieves' earlier crime. One huge metal sculpture was stolen and melted down for its value as scrap metal rather than as art! An unusual heist was carried out by the artist himself. When some thieves broke into a German castle to steal priceless jewels, they certainly wanted to get rich. But, as with many heists, things went wrong.

Let's delve into the shady world of art heists.

This oil painting was found six years after it was stolen in Miami, USA.

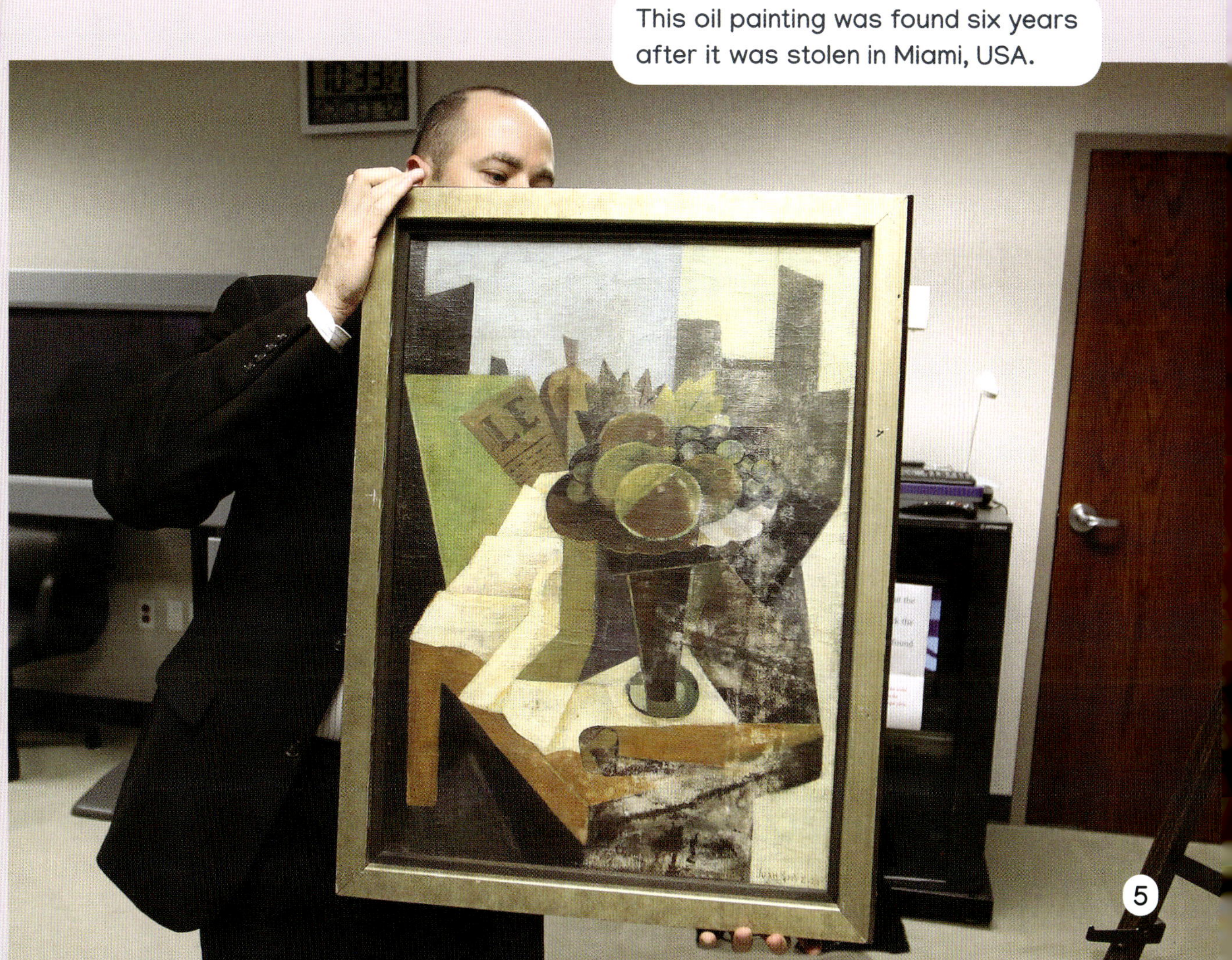

The Mona Lisa

Back in 1911, the *Mona Lisa* was a valuable painting in the Louvre Museum in Paris, France. Since Leonardo da Vinci painted it 400 years earlier, the portrait had been much admired by wealthy people, including French kings and the emperor Napoleon. But it was not well-known to the everyday person. Surprisingly, it was its theft that made the *Mona Lisa* the most famous painting in the world!

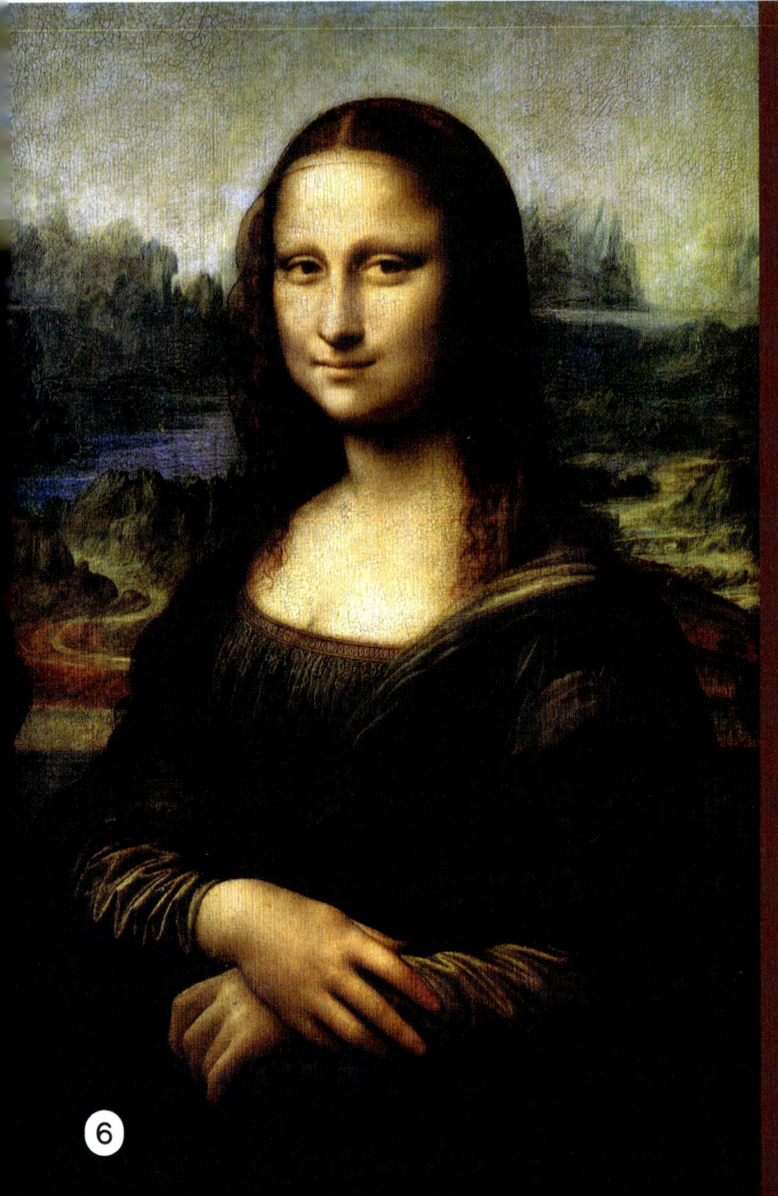

ARTWORK:

Mona Lisa
likely painted 1503–1506

by Leonardo da Vinci
Italian (1452–1519)

Leonardo da Vinci started the painting in 1503 and may have continued refining it for more than 10 years. The portrait is believed to be of Lisa Gheradini, the wife of a wealthy trader in Florence, Italy. The painting is unusual because in those days the **subject** of a portrait did not normally show emotion. Also, women usually posed in richly decorated dresses to indicate their wealth. Neither was the case with the *Mona Lisa*. Her **enigmatic** half-smiling expression hinted at her personality. People today still wonder what she was thinking about!

This heist was carried out by an Italian cabinet maker, Vincenzo Perugia. But it was not planned well in advance. Perugia had been working at the Louvre making glass display cases for some of the paintings. While making the case for the *Mona Lisa*, Perugia had become increasingly annoyed that this Italian masterpiece was being kept in France. He mistakenly believed that Emperor Napoleon had stolen the painting from Italy more than a hundred years earlier. In fact, Leonardo da Vinci had brought the painting to France in the 1500s as a gift for the king.

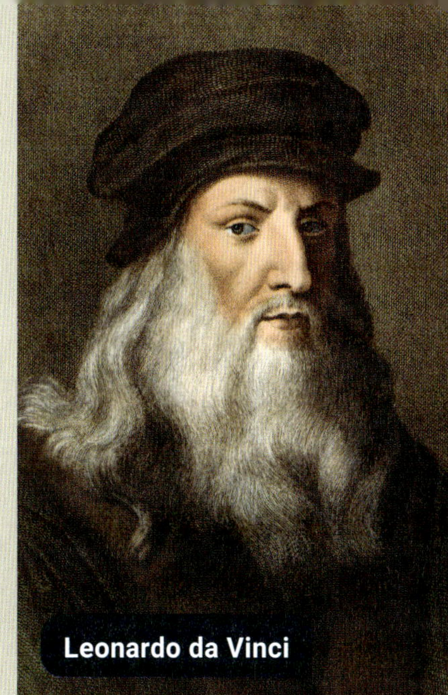
Leonardo da Vinci

This picture shows Vincenzo Perugia and his fingerprints after he was arrested for the theft of the *Mona Lisa*.

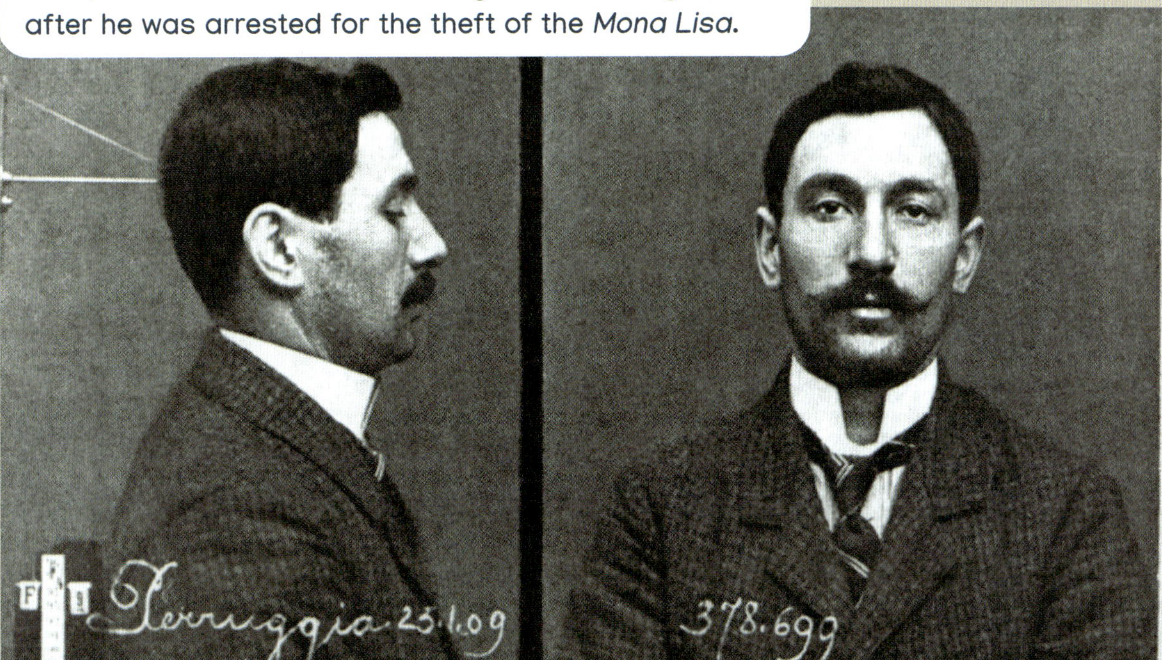

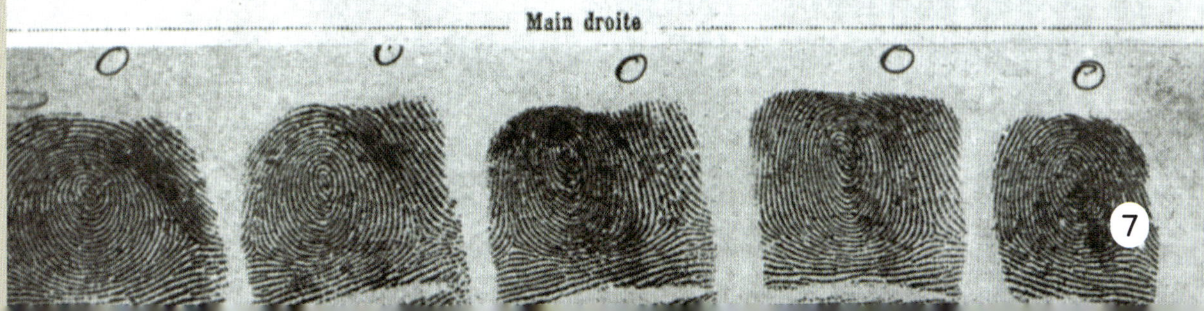

The Louvre was full of art treasures, but museum security was not strict. The guards were mostly old men who had a reputation for napping while on duty. On the morning of 21 August 1911, Perugia pulled the *Mona Lisa* from its hooks on the wall when no one was watching. In a stairwell, he expertly removed the painting from its case and hid it under his coat. Some people think he tried to leave the building from a side door, but it was locked. By chance, a plumber came by with the keys and let Perugia out. The plumber had no idea that Perugia was stealing the *Mona Lisa*!

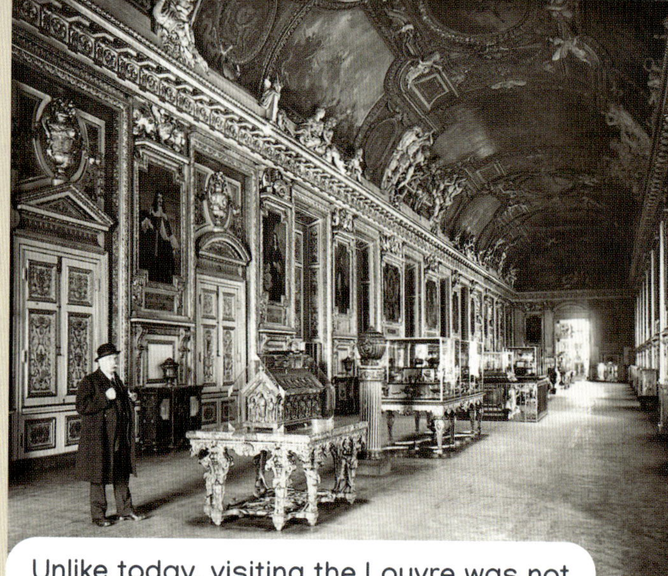

Unlike today, visiting the Louvre was not a popular activity in the early 1900s.

Although Perugia was interviewed by the police and his lodgings were searched, the painting went undiscovered, hidden under a velvet cloth. The police lost interest in Perugia, believing that a poor Italian worker could not have **masterminded** such a theft.

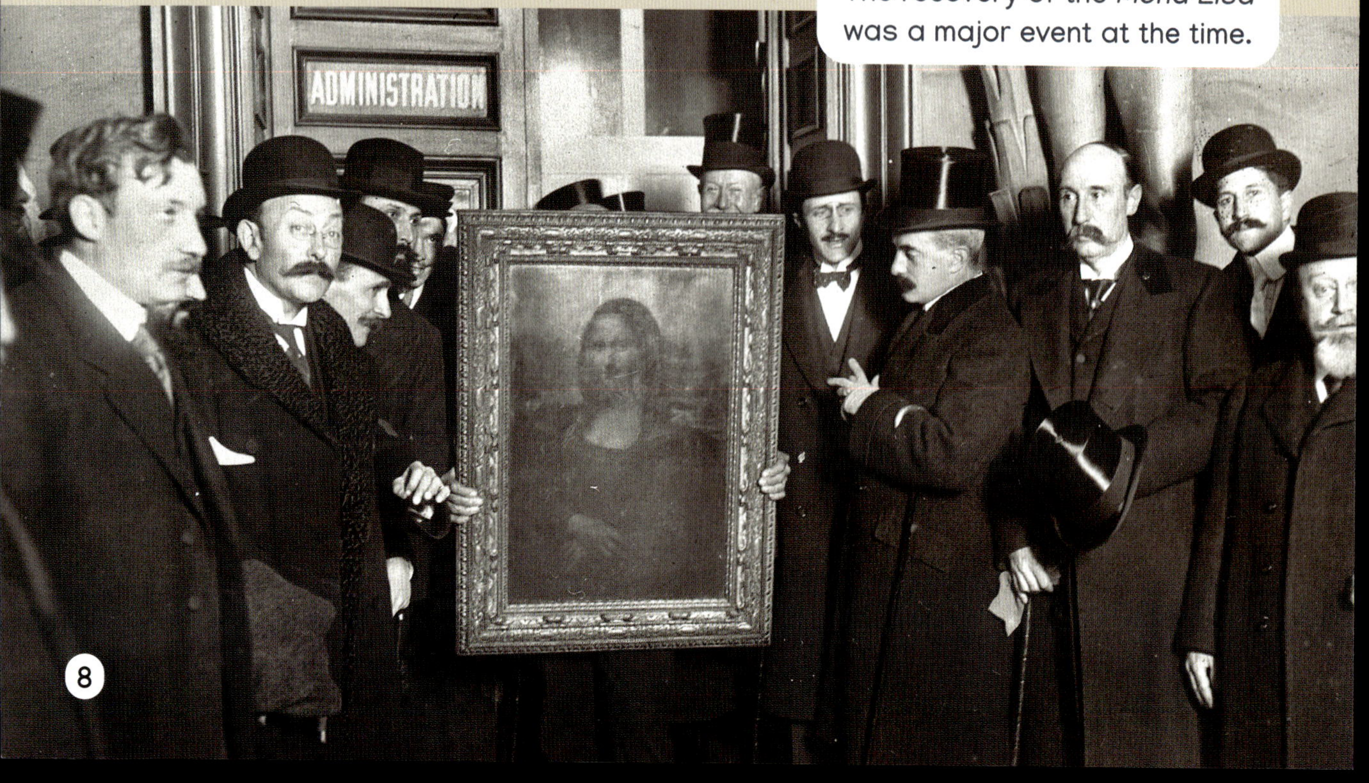

The recovery of the *Mona Lisa* was a major event at the time.

An Unusual Suspect

An up-and-coming young painter named Pablo Picasso became a suspect in the theft of the *Mona Lisa*. Police were convinced that with his background and education, he could have masterminded the heist. But they dropped their investigation when no evidence was found against him. Later, Picasso went on to paint masterpieces of modern art.

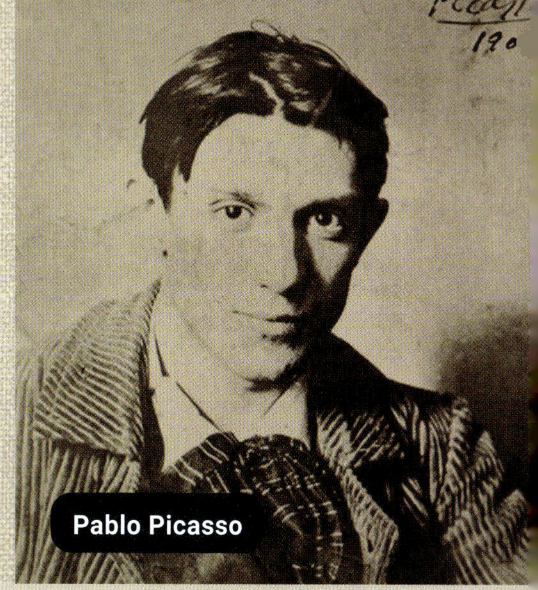

Pablo Picasso

The *Mona Lisa*'s fame grew immediately after the theft. The French public were outraged that this heist could have occurred in their famous museum! The *Mona Lisa* became so famous that dolls and postcards were made of it. Astonishingly, crowds even came to the Louvre to stare at the space on the wall where the painting had once hung!

Today, *Mona Lisa*'s image can be found on a huge range of souvenirs including T-shirts, fridge magnets, posters, glasses cases and fans!

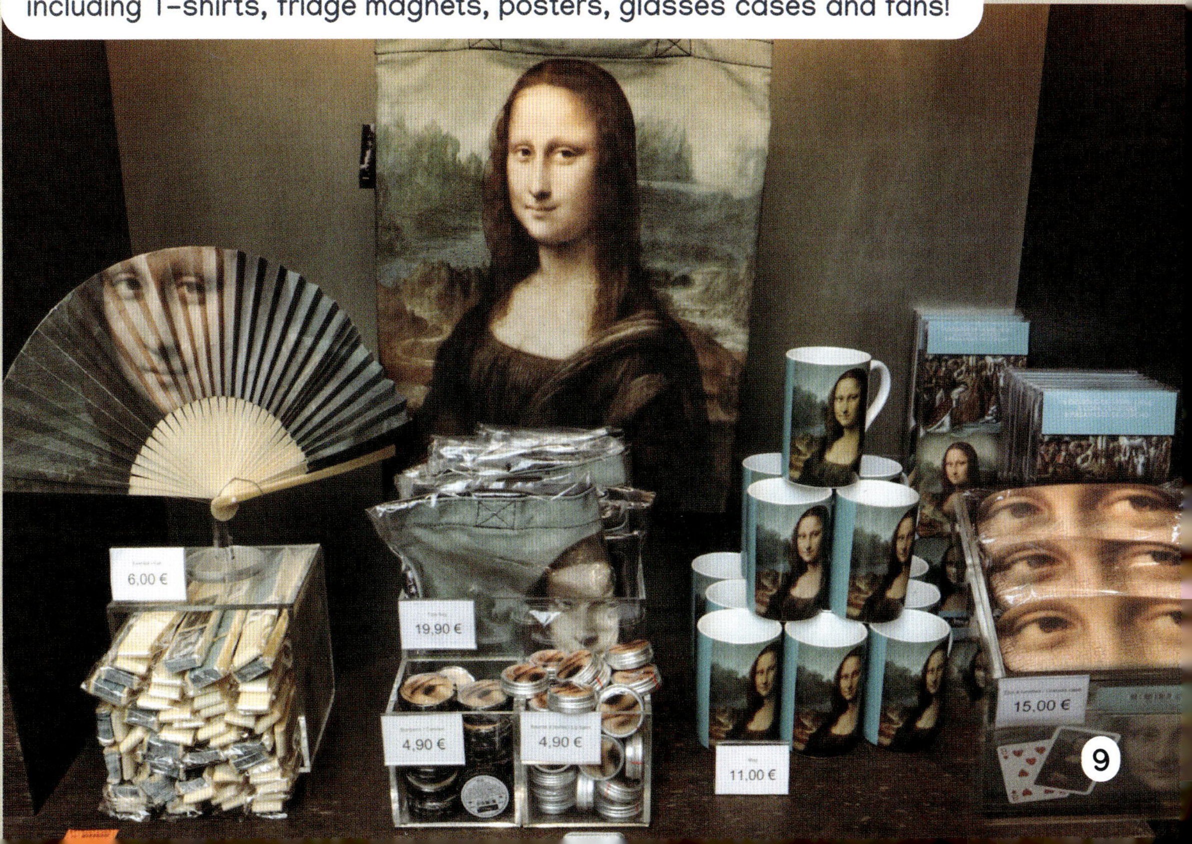

In December 1913, two years after the theft, Perugia offered the *Mona Lisa* to an Italian art dealer. Perugia believed that he would be a hero for returning the painting to Italy. So, he trustingly handed it over to an expert, who took it away to check whether it was real or fake. Instead of getting a reward, as Perugia had expected, the police came and arrested him. The *Mona Lisa* was sent back to the Louvre.

Today, the *Mona Lisa* is kept in a bulletproof glass case in the museum and is seen by about 10 million visitors a year. Many of them go to the Louvre just to see this painting.

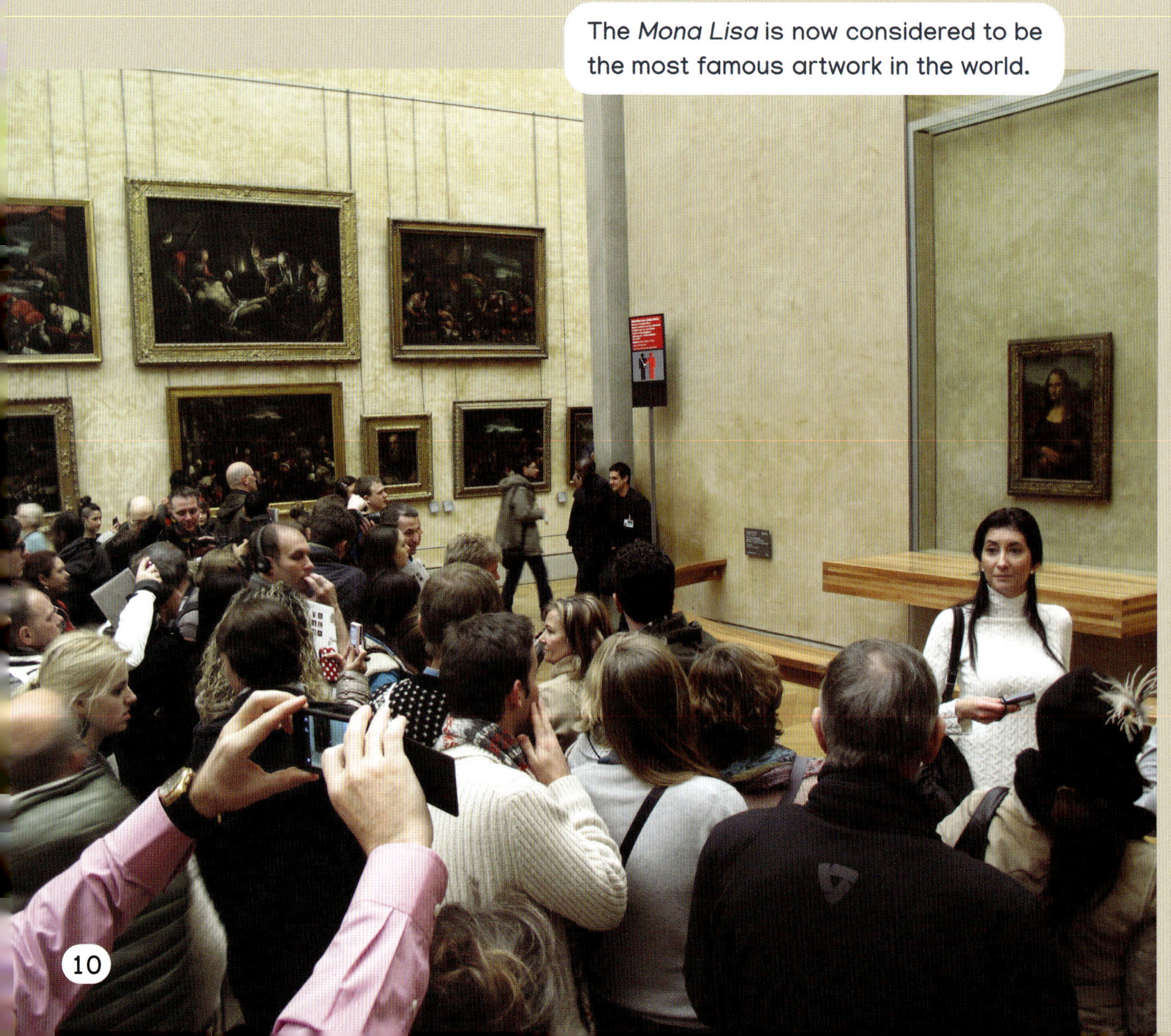

The *Mona Lisa* is now considered to be the most famous artwork in the world.

Weeping Woman

In 1985, the National Gallery of Victoria (NGV) in Melbourne, Australia, acquired *Weeping Woman*, a painting by the famous modern artist Pablo Picasso. It was celebrated by the gallery director as the most important twentieth-century painting in the gallery's collection. However, many people thought it was a wasteful purchase at $1.6 million. It was quite a small painting and modern art was not popular with everyone.

Only seven months later, it was stolen.

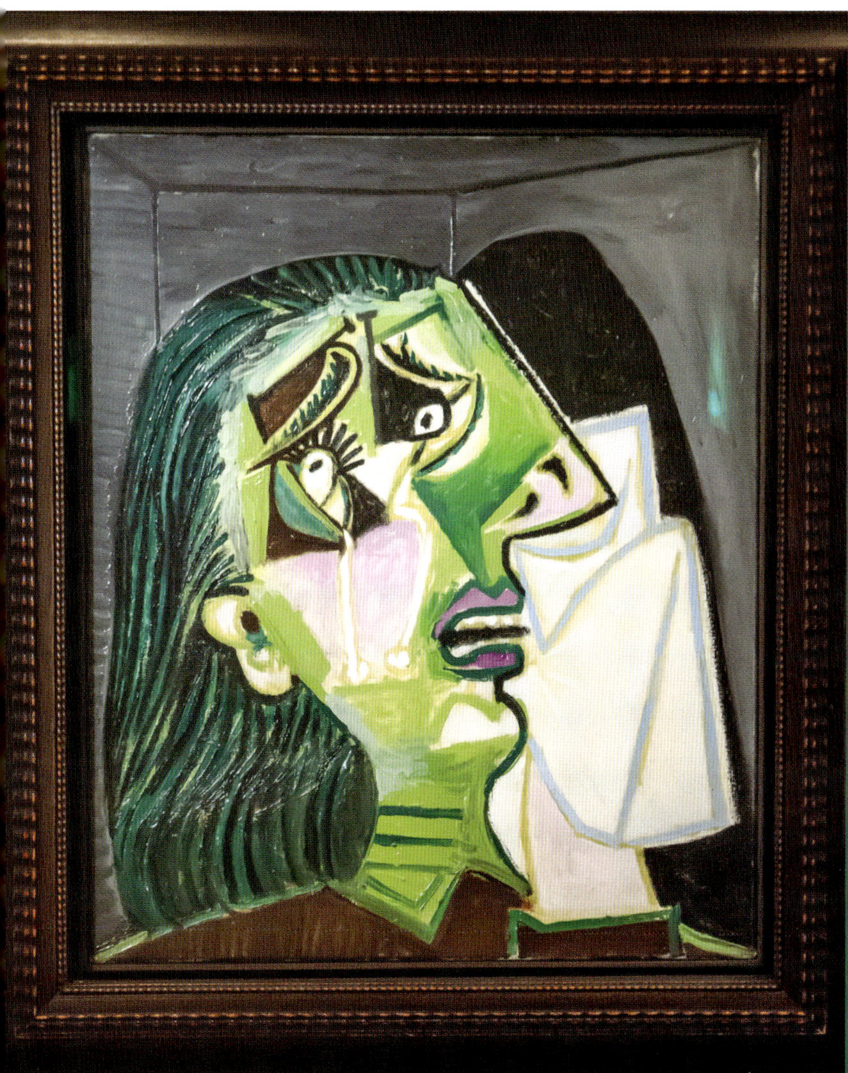

ARTWORK:

Weeping Woman
painted 1937

by Pablo Picasso
Spanish (1881–1973)

Pablo Picasso painted this artwork in 1937. He had created a new style of art called cubism. Picasso painted objects and figures, like the *Weeping Woman*, as **geometric** shapes, often using bright colours.

The heist happened after the gallery closed on Saturday, 2 August 1986. The thieves are thought to have hidden inside the gallery at closing time. Like in the *Mona Lisa* heist, the painting was easily removed from the wall. At that time, new security systems, such as **motion detectors** and **CCTV**, were being installed in other large galleries. But the NGV guards had blocked any such installations, complaining that the cameras would be used to spy on them.

On the following Monday, a letter arrived at *The Age*, a Melbourne newspaper. It stated that a group called the Australian Cultural Terrorists (ACT) had stolen the painting. A journalist then alerted the gallery, which had not yet noticed the theft. The gallery staff and police searched the building for several days. They didn't believe that anyone could have taken the painting from the gallery without being seen.

Copycat Heist?

Pablo Picasso was the artist suspected of stealing the *Mona Lisa* in 1911. Some say this is why his painting was targeted for the Melbourne heist, more than 70 years later.

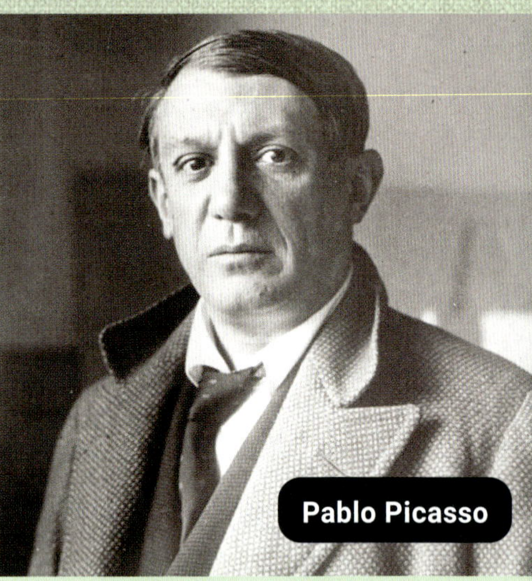

Pablo Picasso

The gallery staff and police checked behind paintings and inside air-conditioning ducts for the missing painting.

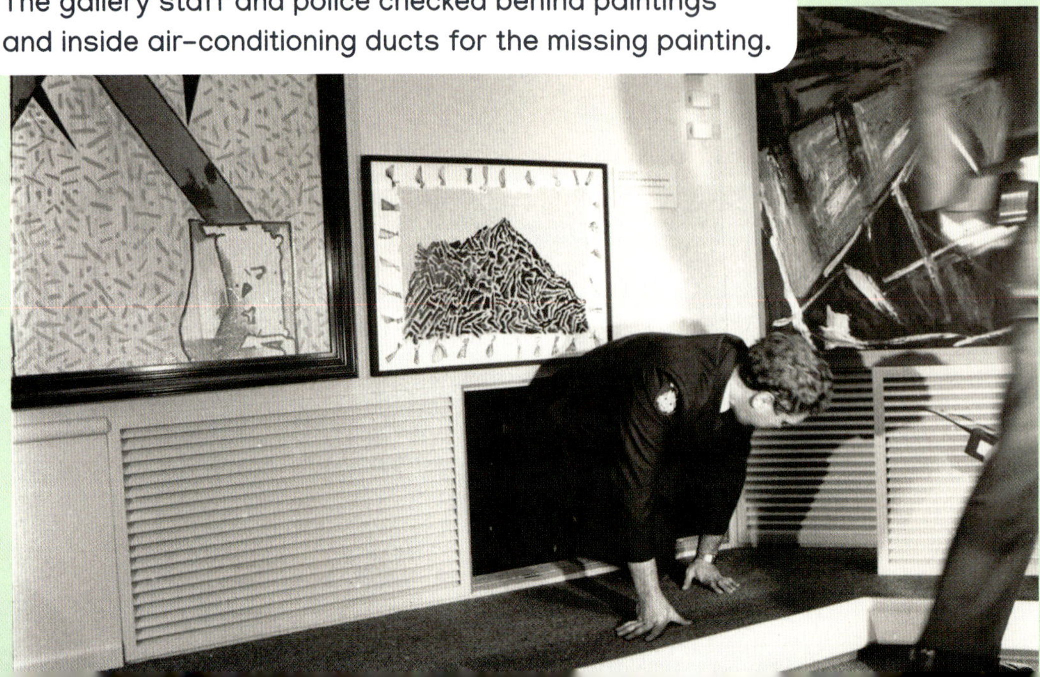

The ACT sent several **ransom notes** to the government minister for the arts, demanding that more funding be given to the arts in Victoria. If not, they threatened to burn the painting. One note included a burnt match!

The ACT's ransom notes were published in the *Age* newspaper.

ATTENTION: RANK MATHEWS (MLA)

We have stolen the Picasso from the National Gallery as a protest against the niggardly funding of the fine arts in this hick State and against the clumsy, unimaginative stupidity of the administration and distribution of that funding.

Two conditions must be publicly agreed upon if the painting is to be returned.

1. The Minister must announce a commitment to increasing the funding of the arts by 10% in real terms over the next three years, and must agree to appoint an independent committee to enquire into the mechanics of the funding of the arts with a view to releasing money from its administration and making it available to artists.

2. The Minister must announce a new annual prize for painting open to artists under thirty years of age. Five prizes of $5000- are to be awarded and the winning paintings acquired for the collection of the National Gallery. A fund is to be established to ensure that the real value of the prizes is maintained each year. The prize is to be called, The Picasso Ransom.

Because the Minister of the Arts is also Minister of Plod, we are allowing him a sporting seven days in which to try to have us arrested while he deliberates. There will be no negotiation. At the end of seven days if our demands have not been met the painting will be destroyed and our campaign continue.

Your very humble servants,

Australian Cultural Terrorists

About two weeks after the theft, *Weeping Woman* was found in a locker at a city train station. It's still not known who the ACT were, but many people suspected they were local artists who had no intention of burning the painting.

After the heist, modern security equipment was installed at the NGV, where the painting remains today.

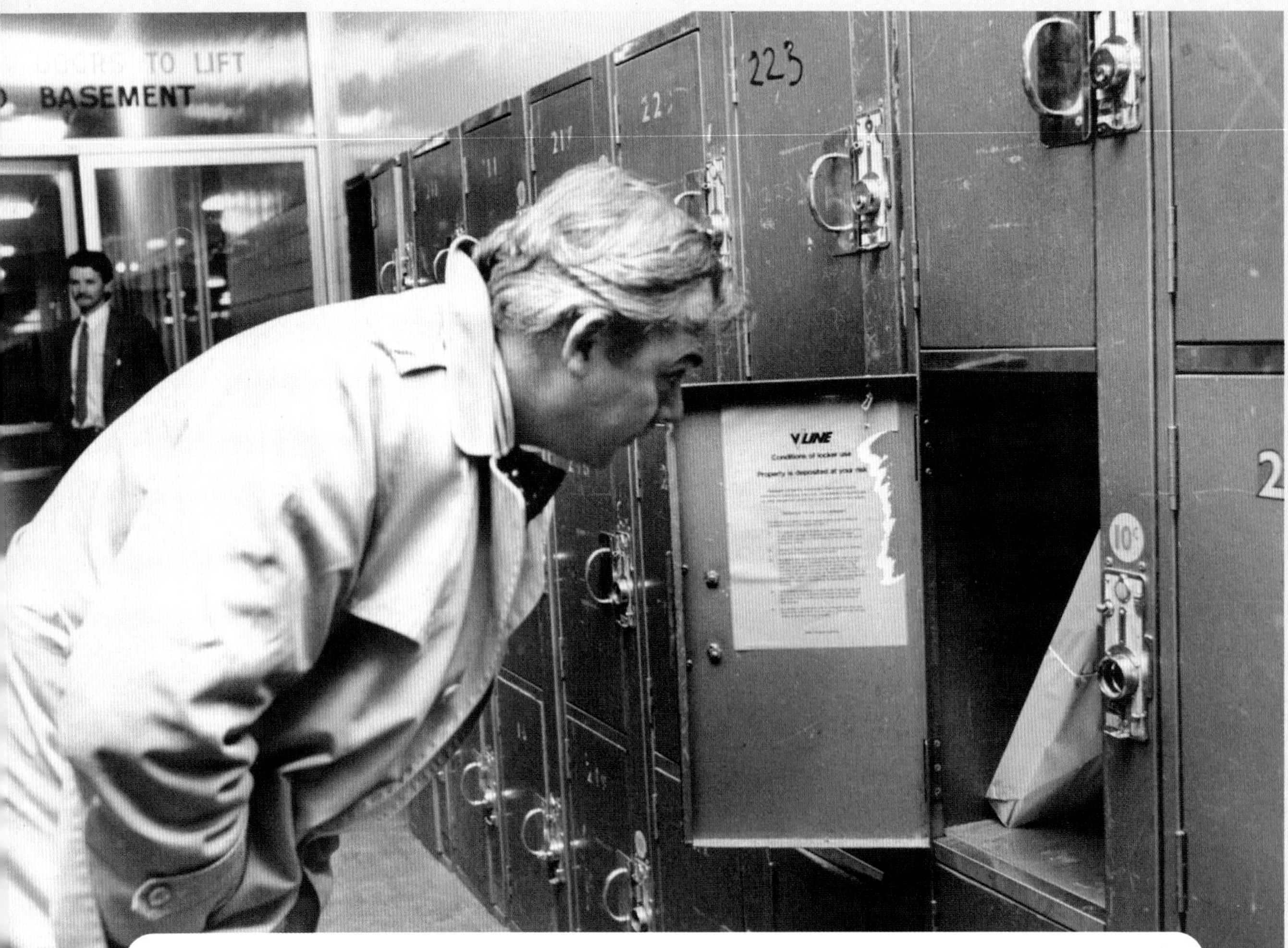

The NGV director was tipped off that the painting was in a locker at Melbourne's Spencer Street Station, today known as Southern Cross Station.

THE SCREAM

Just after 11 am on Sunday, 22 August 2004, two masked thieves entered the Munch (pronounced *Moohnck*) Museum in Oslo, Norway. Visitors were browsing the artworks by the famous Norwegian artist Edvard Munch, including his modern art masterpiece *The Scream*.

One thief, who was carrying a weapon, ordered the visitors and two guards to lie on the floor. The other thief pulled *The Scream* off the wall. No alarms went off, and on their way out the thieves even managed to pull another painting from a wall!

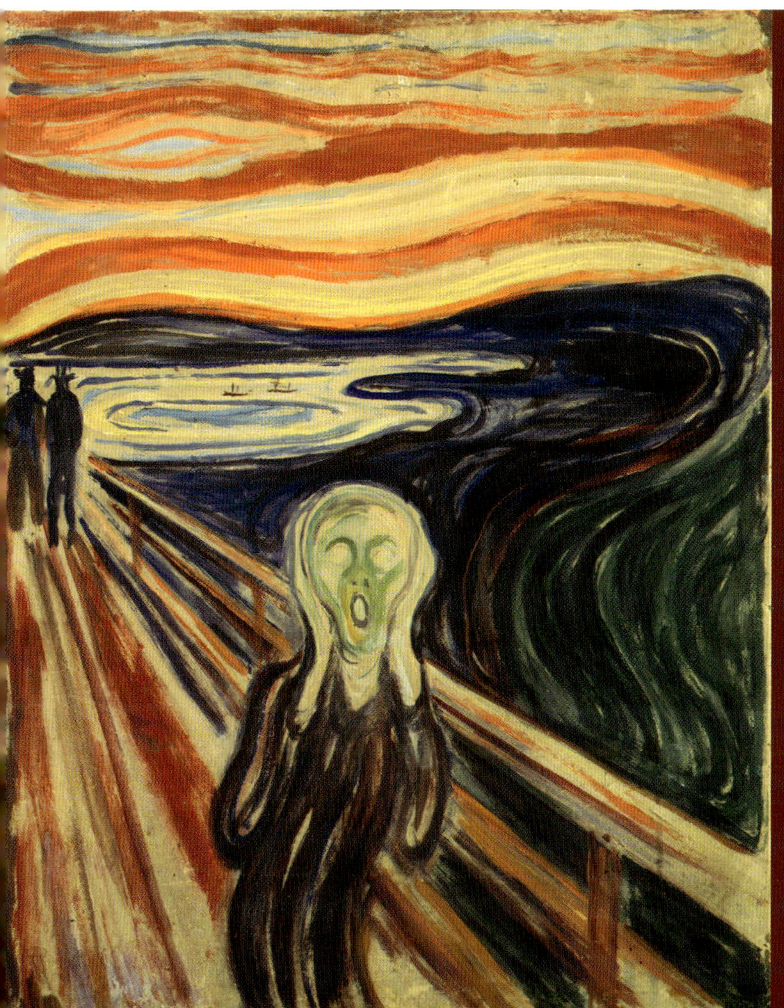

ARTWORK:

The Scream
painted 1910

by Edvard Munch
Norwegian (1863–1944)

Edvard Munch painted *The Scream* in 1910. He is famous for painting in an **abstract** style of modern art from the early 1900s known as expressionism. The shapes and colours of the painting are distorted and exaggerated to express a mood or effect, rather than to show reality.

Shocked witnesses said that the clumsy thieves had dropped the paintings as they fled the museum. Then, outside in the street, a passer-by took a photo of the thieves running to a waiting getaway car.

The police later found the car, along with some broken pieces of frame and glass from the paintings. Norwegians feared that their treasured artworks had been damaged in the heist. The investigation trail went quiet for a while, as no ransom note was received.

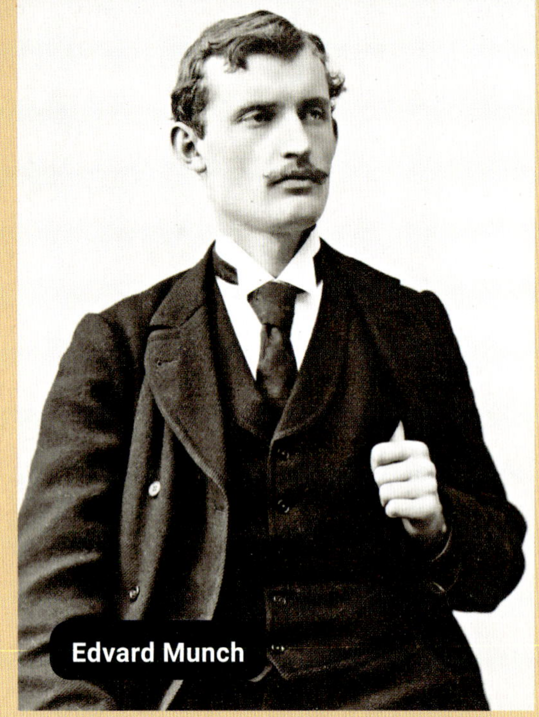

Edvard Munch

Several people were suspected of being involved in the heist, and a getaway car was parked outside the museum.

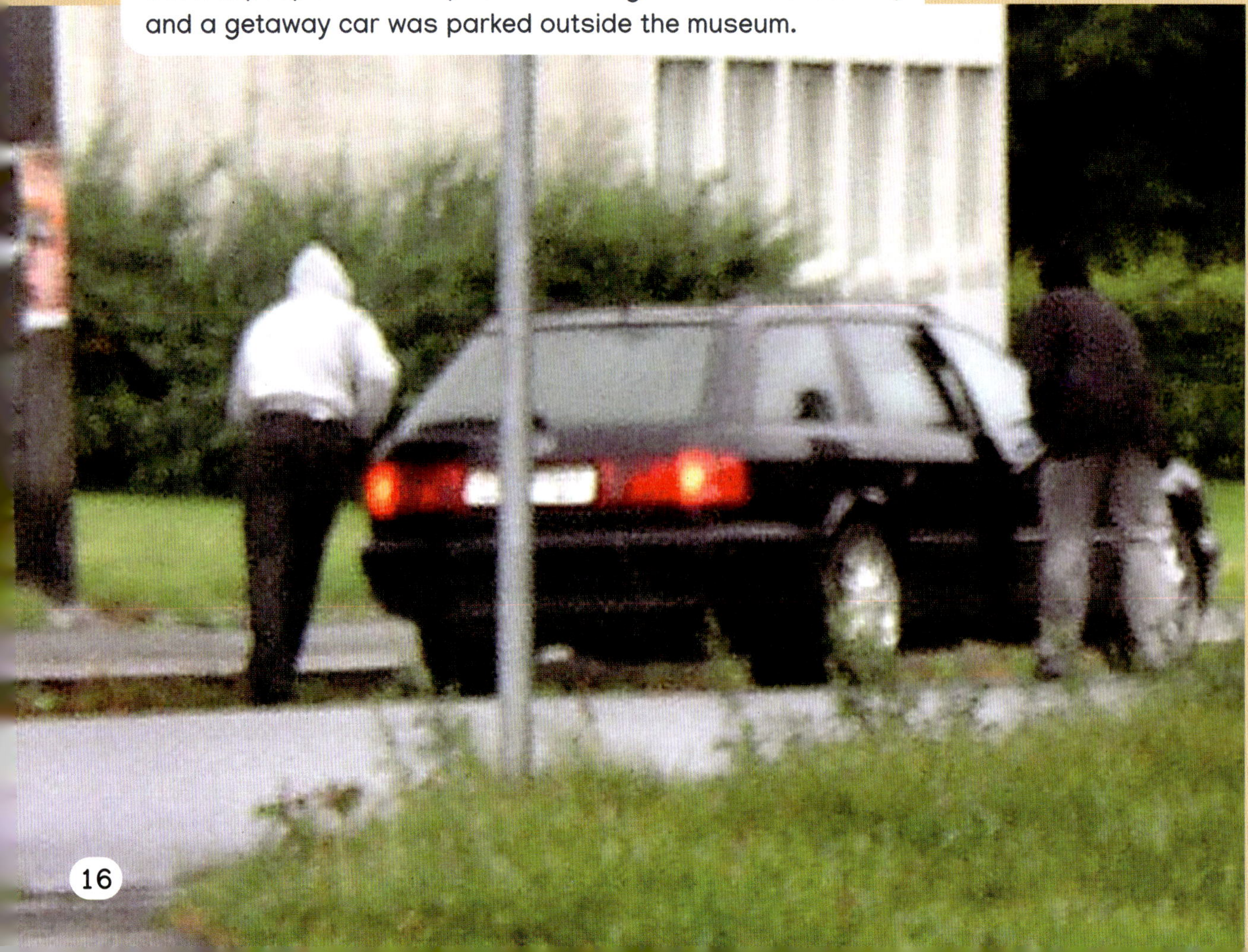

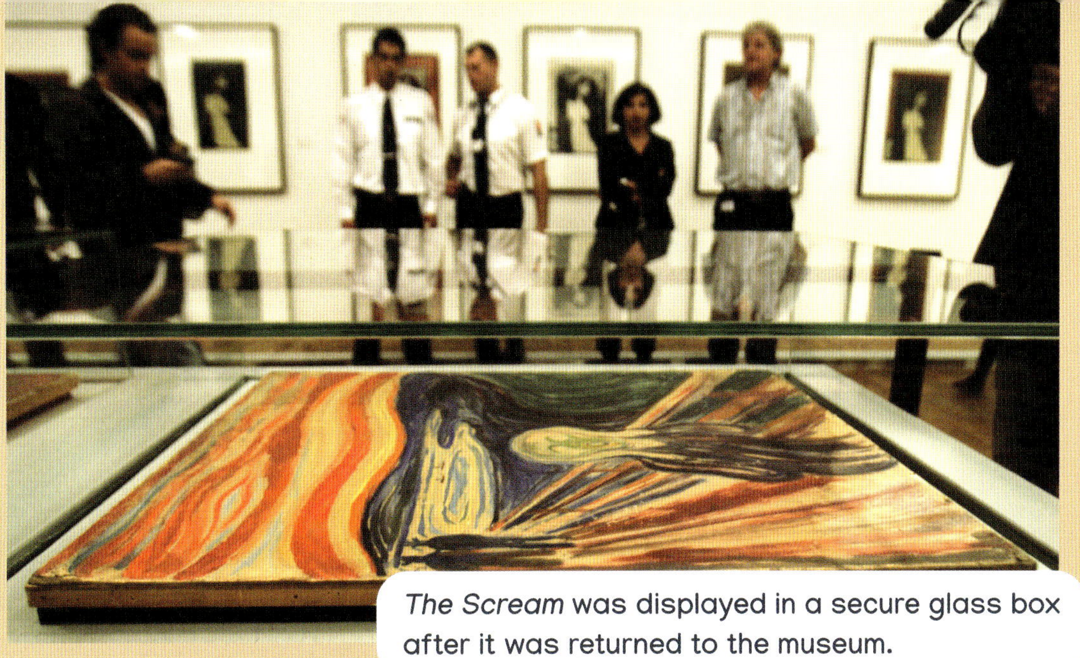

The Scream was displayed in a secure glass box after it was returned to the museum.

In May 2006, three men were convicted of planning the heist and driving and supplying the getaway car. Three others, including one suspected thief, were **acquitted**. There was still no sign of the paintings. Then, in August 2006, they were found with only minor damage.

So why did the thieves want the paintings? The police didn't provide many details about the crime. Some people think that the gang wanted to distract police from investigating an earlier crime. It has also been suggested that someone in jail gave police the information about where to find the paintings – they may even have received a reward!

MULTIPLE SCREAMS!

Munch made several versions of this artwork: two paintings, some drawings and some prints, all called *The Scream*, but all slightly different. In 1994, the other painting of *The Scream* was stolen from the National Gallery of Oslo, but it was returned within three months. The audacious thieves had left a note pinned to the wall, thanking the museum for its poor security!

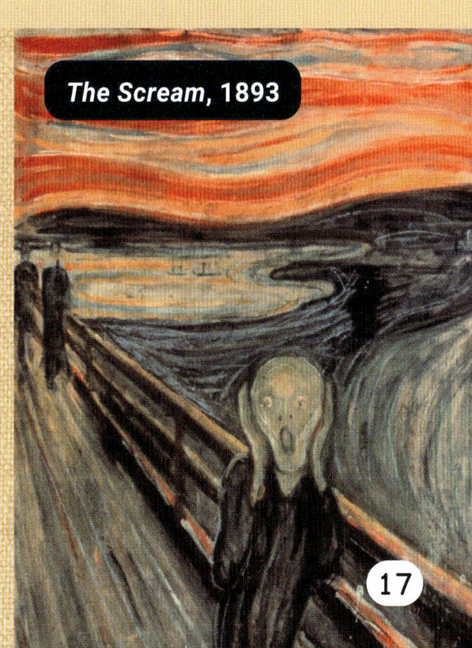

***The Scream*, 1893**

Reclining Figure

Some artworks are large and heavy, like Henry Moore's *Reclining Figure* sculptures. So it was quite a shock when one of these huge sculptures was stolen from a park in England owned by the artist's family.

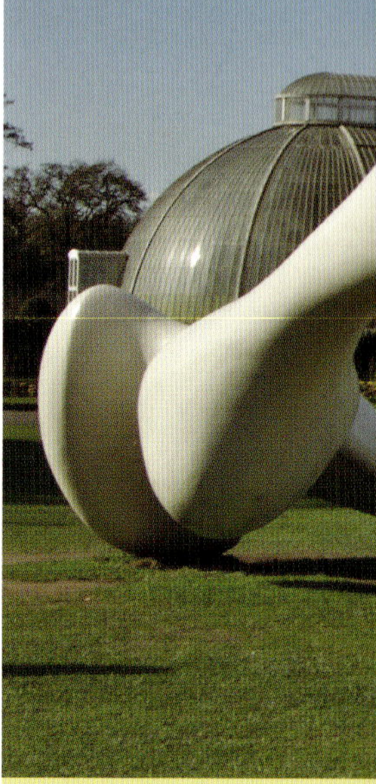

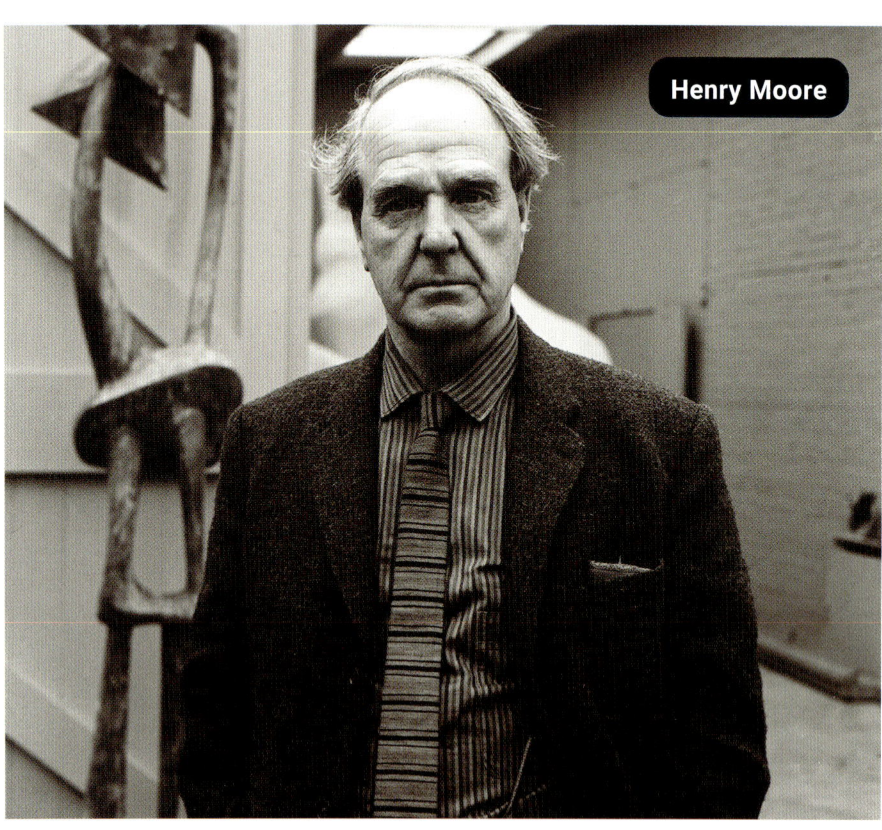

Henry Moore

ARTWORK:

Reclining Figure
sculpted 1969–1970

by Henry Moore
British (1898–1986)

Henry Moore was particularly famous for large abstract-style sculptures, which often show people sitting or lying down. He had six bronze statues made of the *Reclining Figure*: five for international display and one for himself.

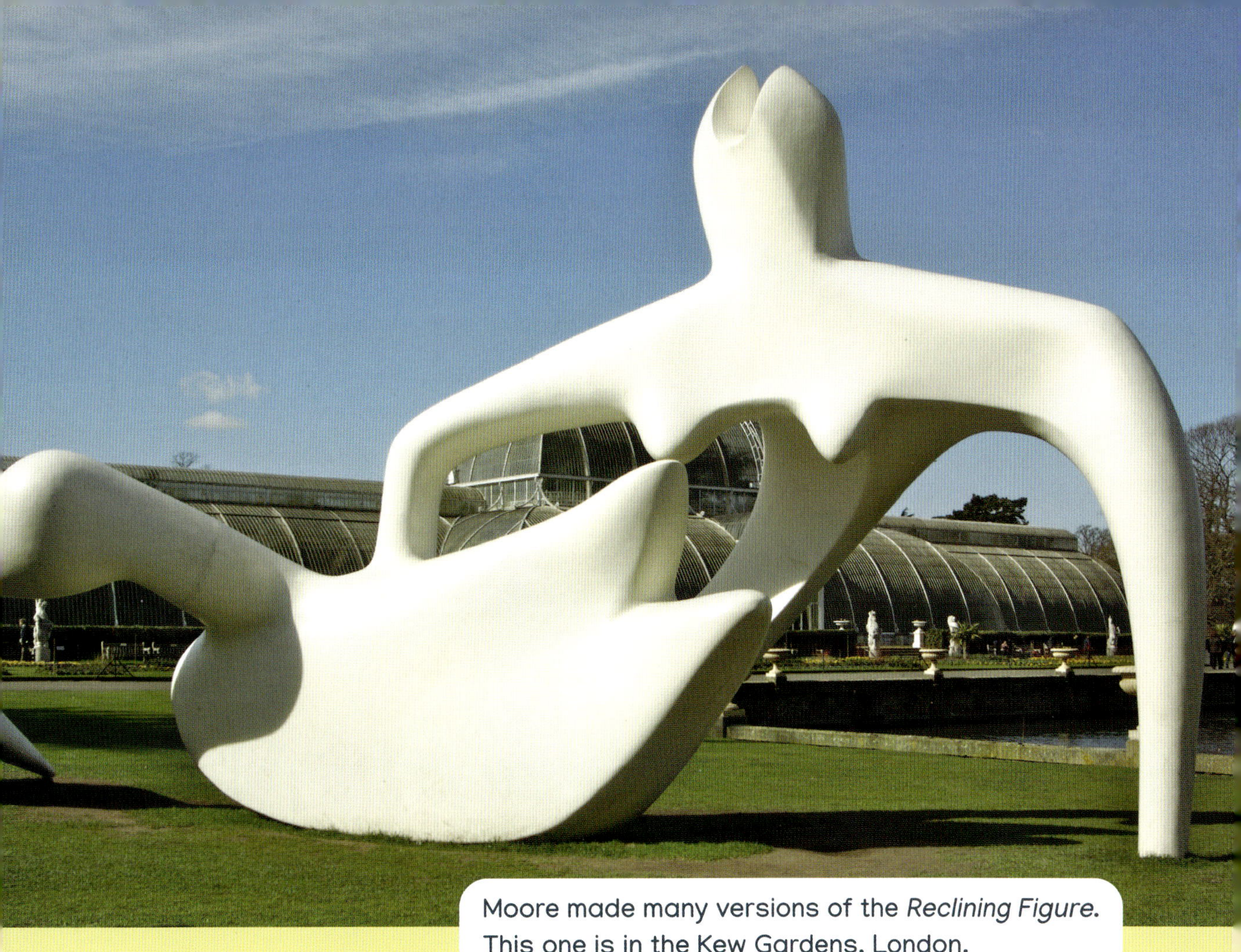

Moore made many versions of the *Reclining Figure*. This one is in the Kew Gardens, London.

The theft took place during the night of 15 December 2005. Police thought that a clever gang of thieves had planned and carried out the heist. They would have needed a crane and a large truck to remove the two-tonne sculpture! At that time, it was worth about 3 million British pounds.

At first, people wondered if a private art collector had arranged the heist: who else would want such a distinctive and large item? Police alerted Europe's shipping ports to be on the lookout, in case the thieves tried to ship the sculpture out of Europe.

But after more investigations, the police found evidence that the sculpture was most likely cut up and melted down for scrap metal. The thieves were never caught and might not have known the artwork's true value. They would only have received about 1500 pounds for the scrap metal.

Girl with Balloon

This heist was very unusual – it was carried out by the artist on his own artwork! The mysterious street artist known as Banksy became famous for his stencilled murals. His most famous one was *Girl with Balloon*. It appeared on a London street in 2002. But the artwork at the centre of this unusual heist was a rare spray-painted, framed version.

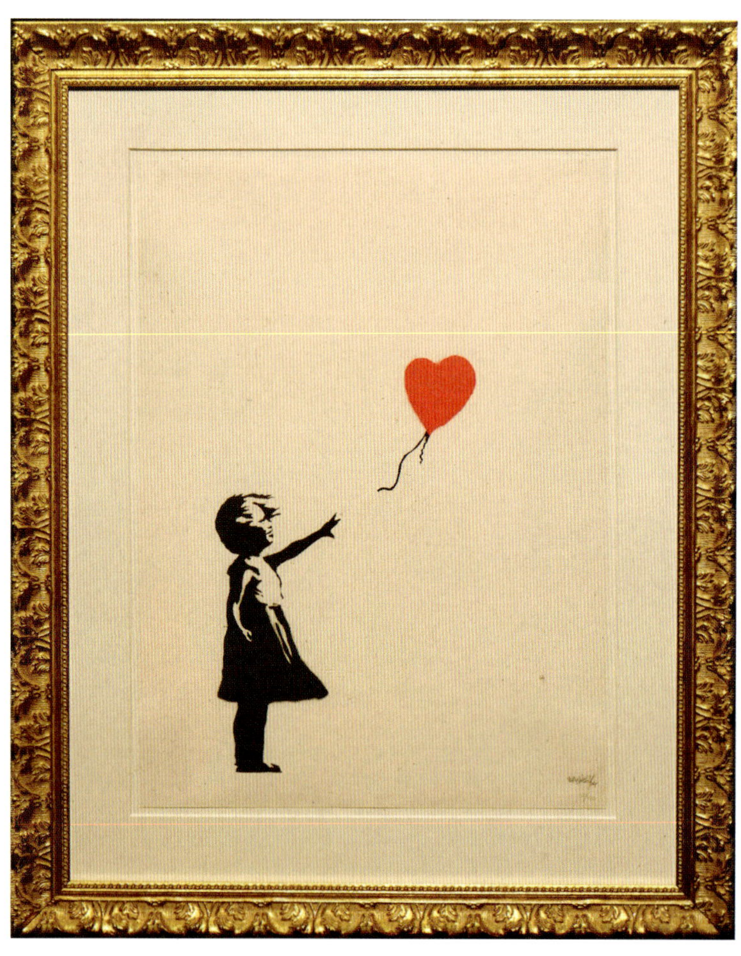

ARTWORK:

Girl with Balloon
created 2002

by Banksy
United Kingdom

In 2006, Banksy recreated *Girl with Balloon* as a painting and gave it to a friend. The simple image of a young girl and a heart-shaped balloon has become an icon of a style of art known as street art. For his murals, Banksy uses stencils and spray paint so he can quickly complete his artwork without attracting attention in the street. Even today, Banksy's identity is a closely kept secret!

On 5 October 2018, the painting was sold for over $1.5 million at an art auction. Immediately after the sale, the painting slid down inside its frame and began to be shredded! The shredder jammed, leaving half of the painting **intact**. Onlookers were stunned. Who was responsible for such an audacious act? It had robbed the buyer of their newly purchased artwork.

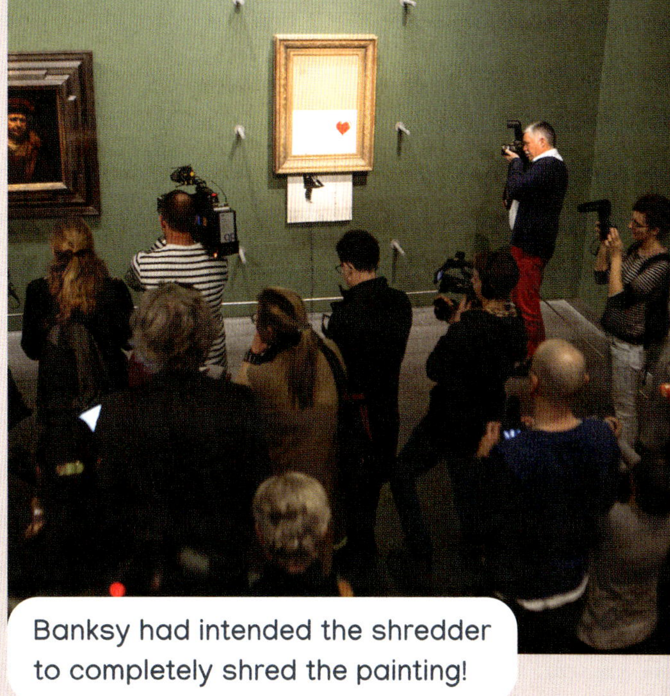

Banksy had intended the shredder to completely shred the painting!

After the auction, Banksy wrote on social media that he had built the shredder into the frame of the painting years earlier, just in case the painting was ever sold at auction.

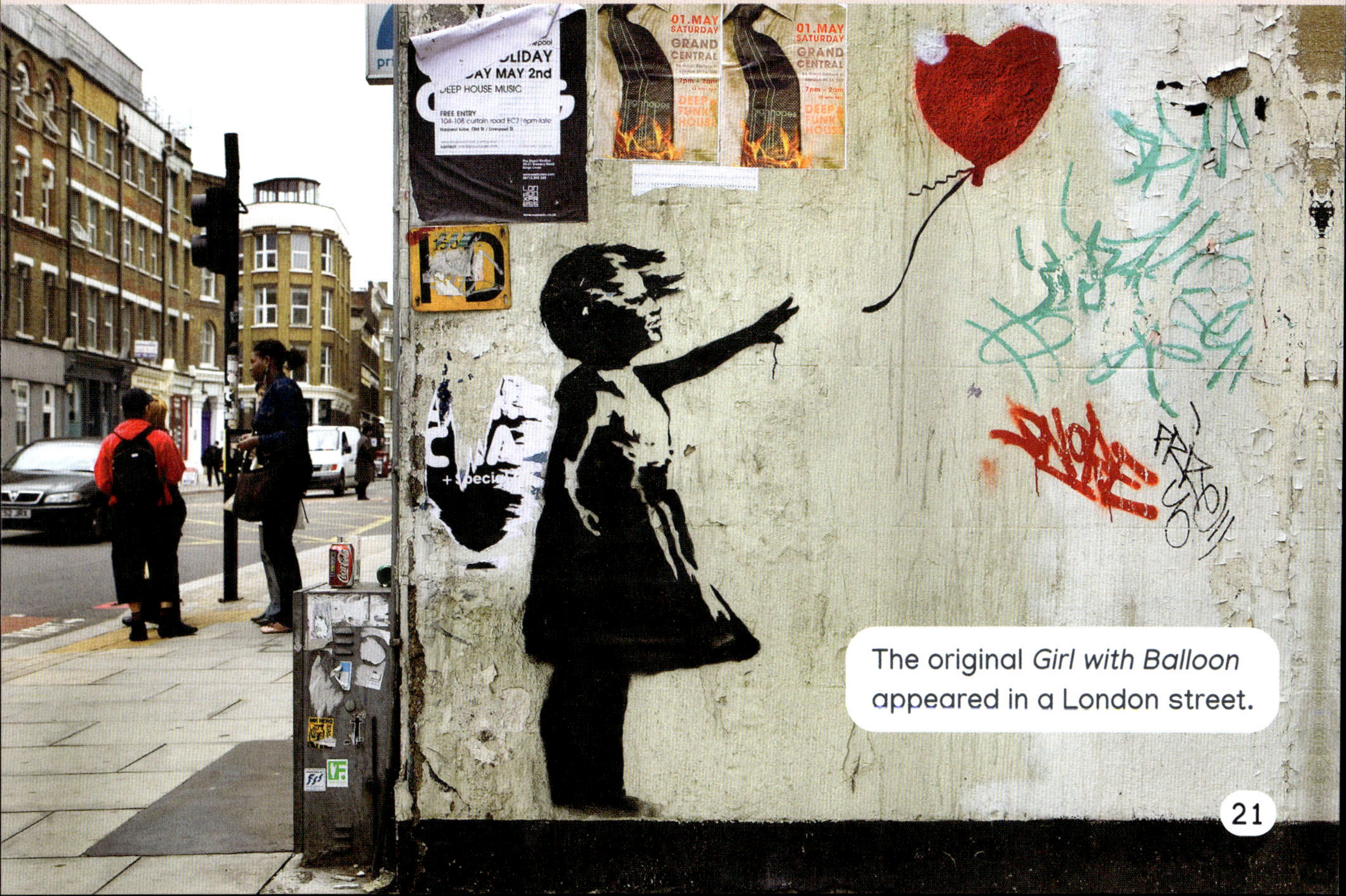

The original *Girl with Balloon* appeared in a London street.

But why had Banksy destroyed his own artwork? It was as a protest. He hated the idea of his artworks being sold for high prices, explaining that this was why he put them in public places. But that didn't stop people from paying large sums for his art. People had already begun to remove pieces of wall containing his murals to sell them.

Banksy also wrote that he had renamed the painting *Love in the Bin*. It has since been sold at auction in its semi-shredded state. Amazingly, the value of the artwork is now much higher than if it hadn't been shredded!

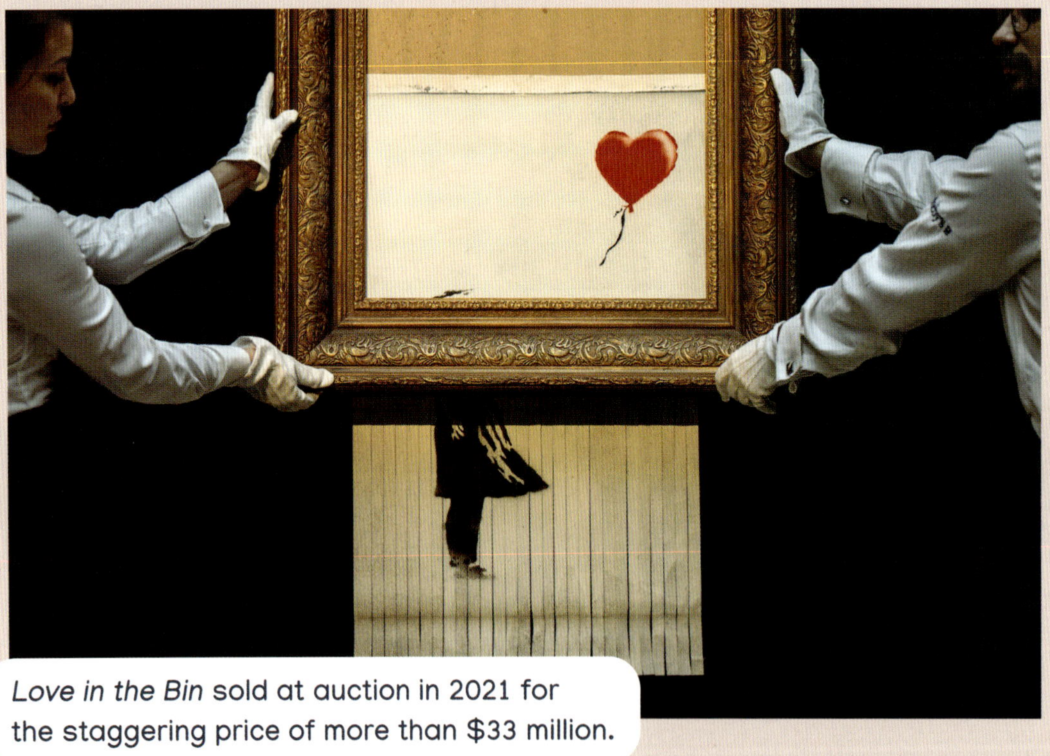

Love in the Bin sold at auction in 2021 for the staggering price of more than $33 million.

Heist or Prank?

Banksy had a history of performing pranks that poked fun at traditional ideas about art. In 2004, he sneakily stuck his own framed version of the *Mona Lisa* up on a wall in the Louvre. Banksy had replaced *Mona Lisa*'s enigmatic expression with a yellow smiley face!

The Green Vault

The Green Vault is a series of rooms built in Dresden Castle in Germany in the 1500s. In the early 1700s, Augustus II, known as Augustus the Strong, was the Ruler of **Saxony** and King of Poland. He decided to use these rooms to house his treasures. Augustus's **descendants** continued to add to the collection. The Green Vault contains jewellery, and artworks made of gold, silver and sparkling gemstones, including the Dresden Green Diamond: the largest green diamond ever found!

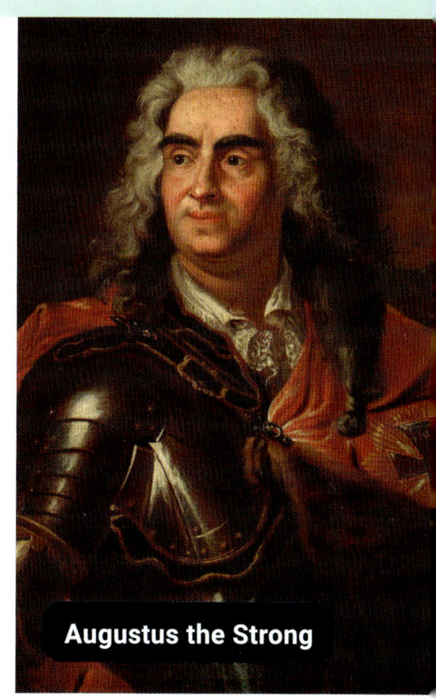
Augustus the Strong

ARTWORKS:

The Green Vault
Dresden Castle, 1700s

Augustus II the Strong
King of Poland,
Ruler of Saxony

Augustus turned the Green Vault into a museum so that the people of Saxony could marvel at their artistic heritage. The vault itself is a masterpiece of decoration, and many of the artworks were made by top German craftspeople and artists from the 1700s.

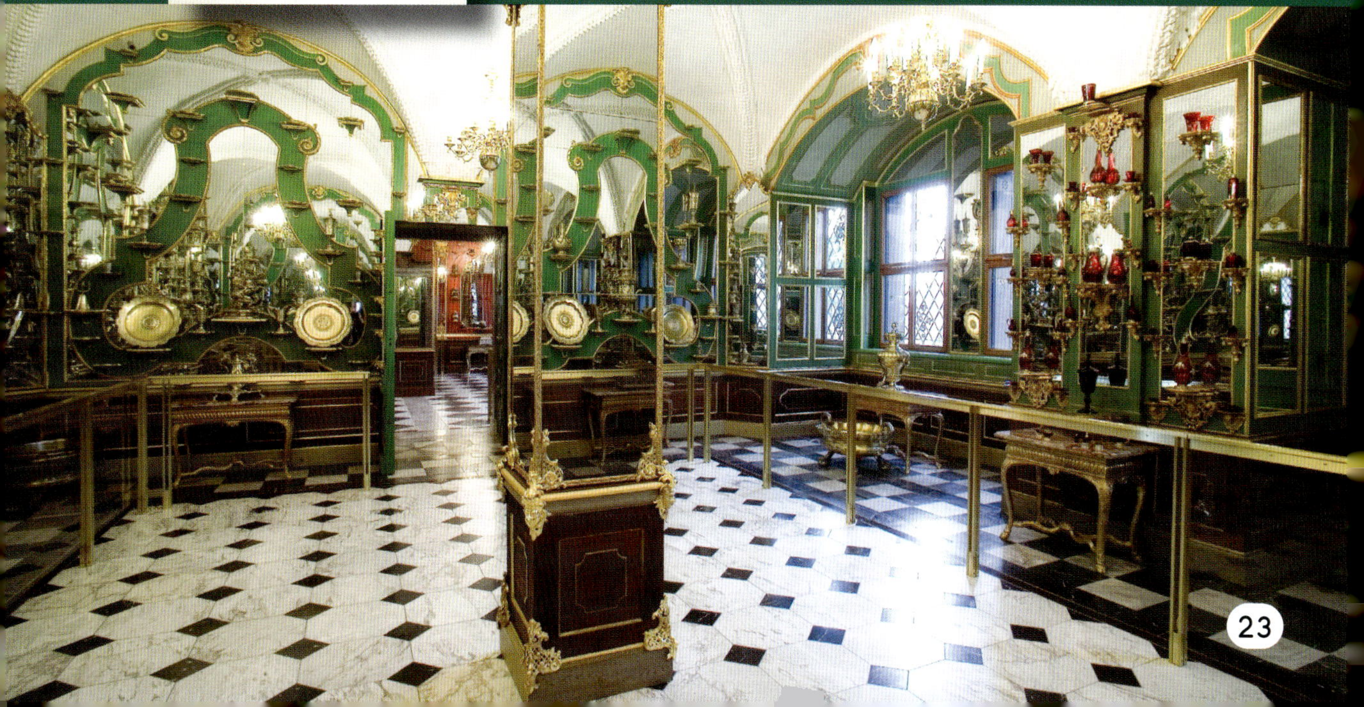

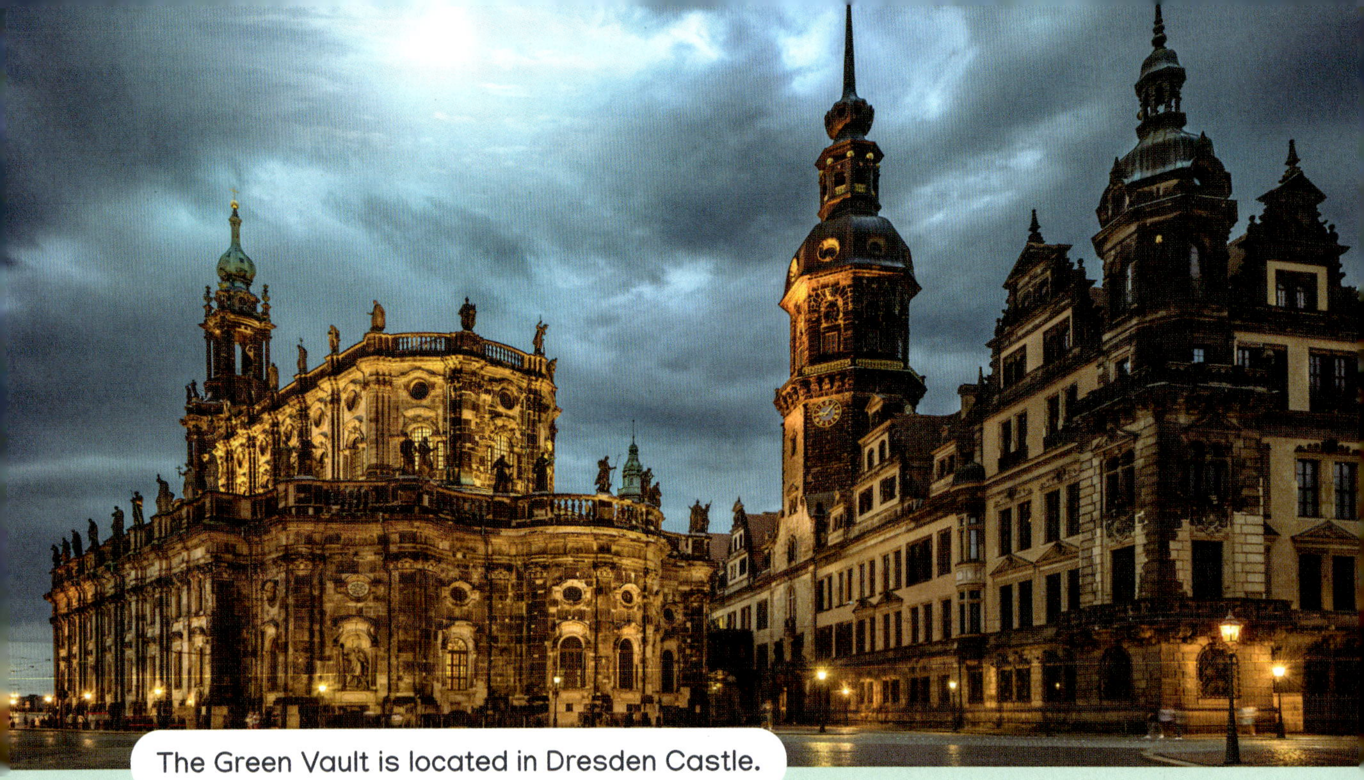

The Green Vault is located in Dresden Castle.

The Green Vault was thought to be **impregnable**, until it was targeted by a gang of criminals in November 2019.

A few months earlier, the gang began preparing for the heist. They **scoped out** the streets around the palace, looking for the best escape route, and acquired getaway cars. One of the criminals stole a Jaws of Life machine from a tool factory. This machine is normally used for pulling apart heavy metal pieces in road accidents to remove people from damaged vehicles.

A Bit Late!

Police investigated the theft of the Jaws of Life. The criminal had left his **DNA** at the factory crime scene and was arrested for the theft two days after the Green Vault heist.

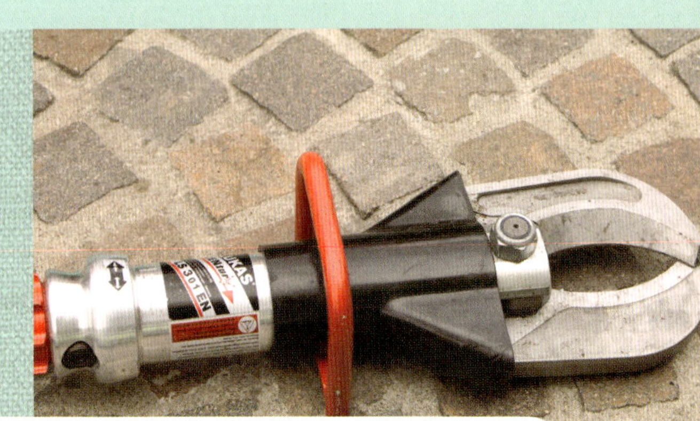

The Jaws of Life machine is a very strong tool that can pull metal apart.

Two nights before the heist, the thieves cut the thick metal security **grille** covering a small window to the museum, probably using the Jaws of Life. Then, they fixed the grille back into position, so that no one would notice it.

The day before the heist, the gang visited the museum, posing as visitors. They closely inspected one of the glass cases in the Chamber of Jewels, a room inside the Green Vault. They also stopped to look at the small window with the security grille. This visit was only discovered after the heist, when the authorities checked the CCTV footage from that day.

The precious jewels stolen from the Green Vault were in glass cases like these ones.

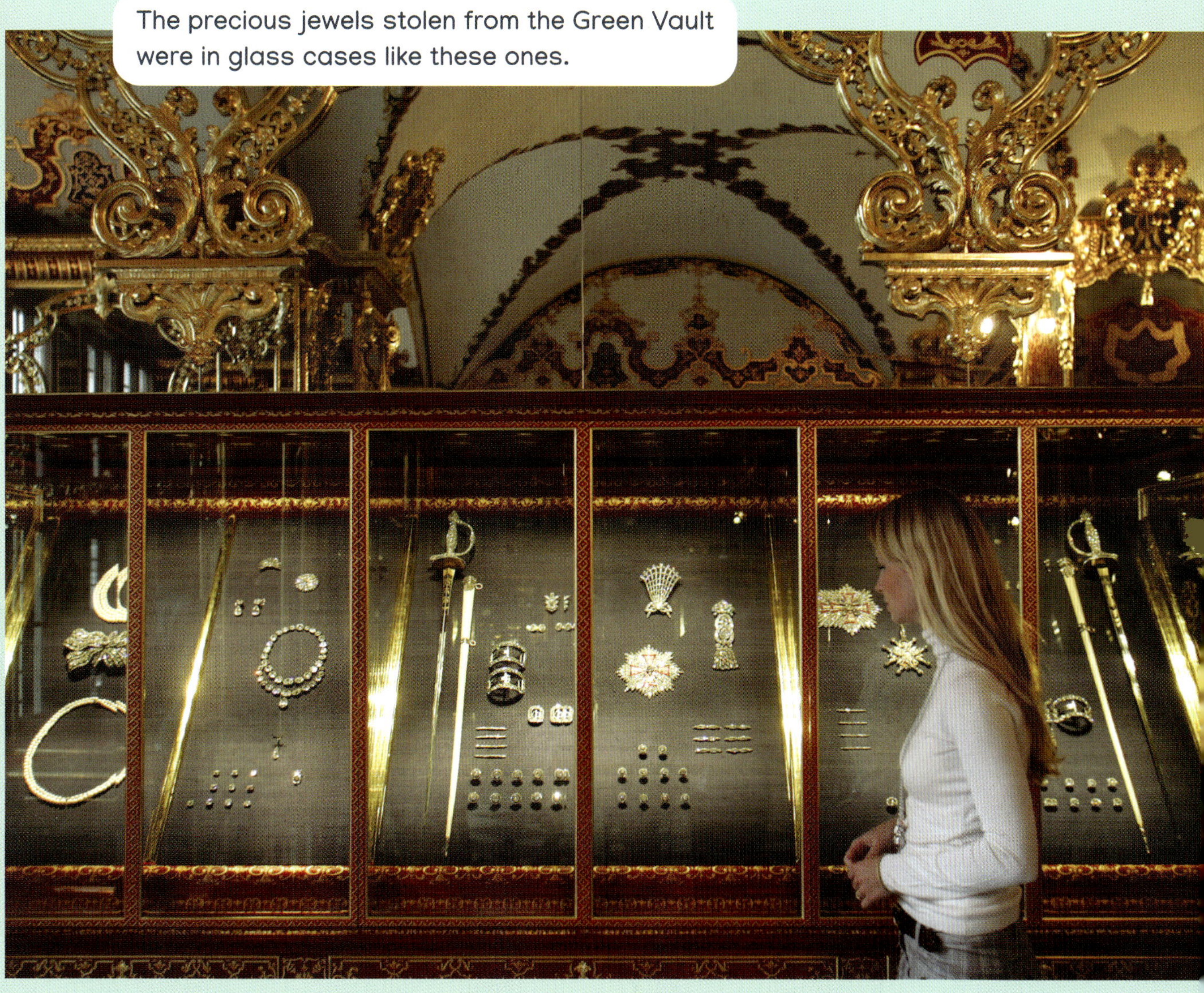

At about 4:50 am on 25 November, a fire was detected in a local electrical supply box near the museum. It blacked out lights in the neighbourhood. Inside the museum, the security cameras still worked, but the rooms of the vault were now in darkness.

Around the same time, two gang members removed the pre-cut security grille on the small window and climbed into the museum. The motion detectors didn't work, so the thieves could head straight for the Chamber of Jewels without setting off any alarms.

At 4:57 am, two museum security guards noticed the thieves using torches to find their way around the vault. The shocked guards immediately reported the robbery to the police. The guards did not carry weapons and could only watch on helplessly as the thieves smashed glass cases and stole millions of dollars' worth of jewels.

The thieves emptied many display cases such as this one.

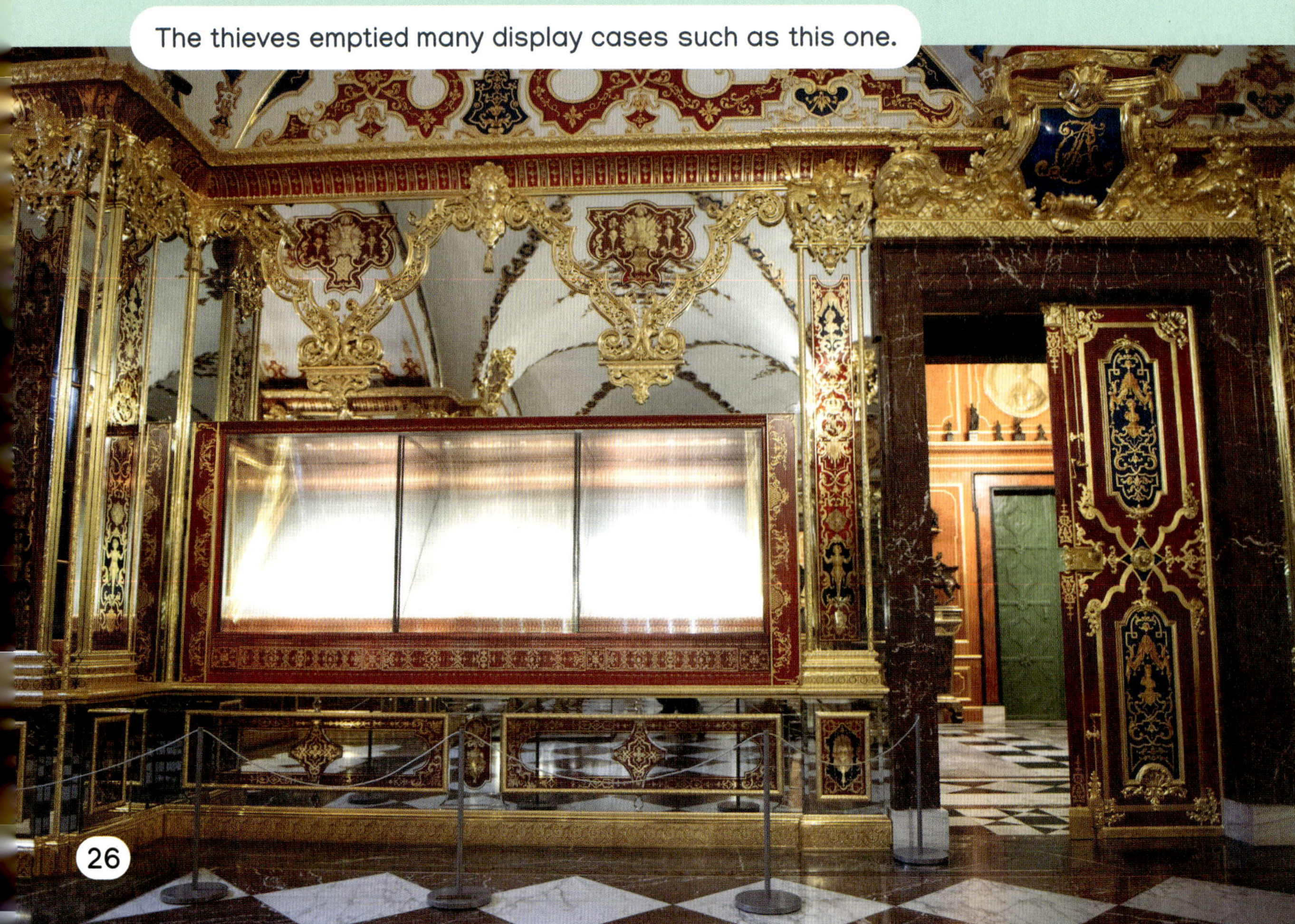

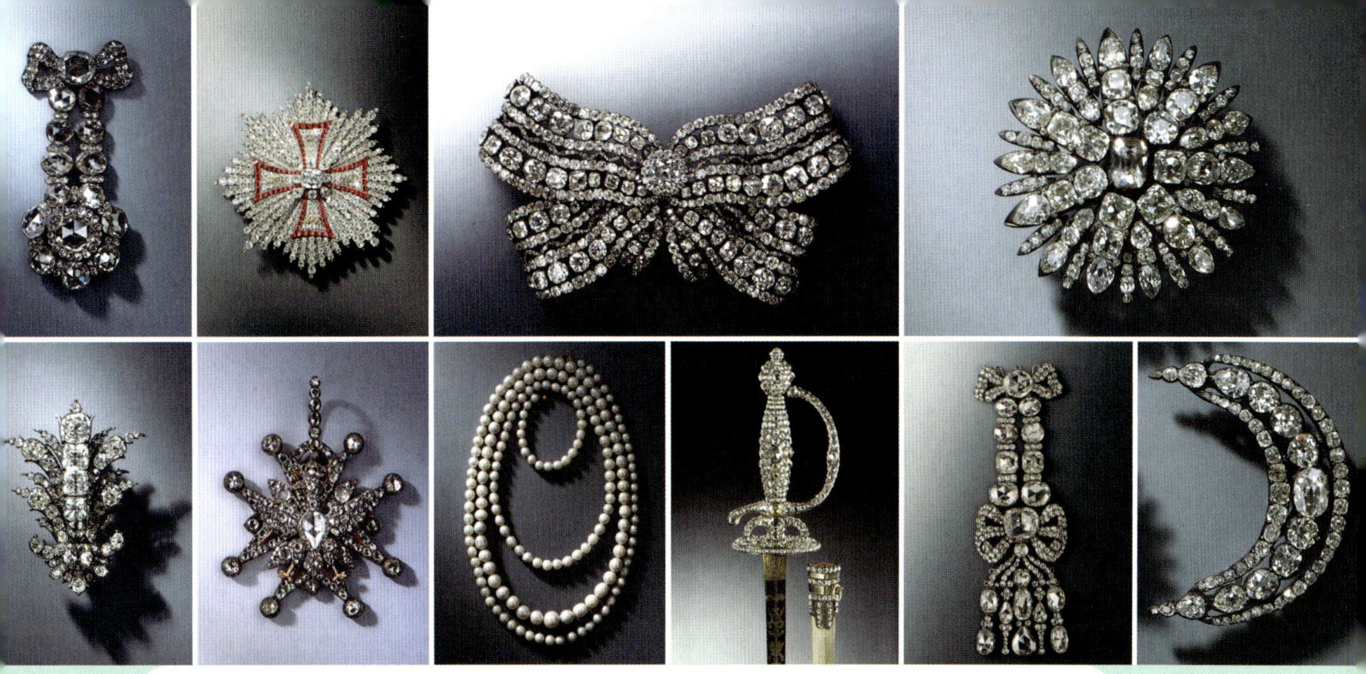

These valuable items were among those stolen from the Green Vault.

The police arrived about 9 minutes after the thieves had broken into the vault. But the thieves and the jewels were gone. A burnt-out getaway car was found later, with no traces of DNA that might link the gang members to the heist.

The thieves stole necklaces, brooches and rings that had once been worn by Augustus and his descendants. They also took jewelled military badges and awards, and a sword with a diamond-covered hilt.

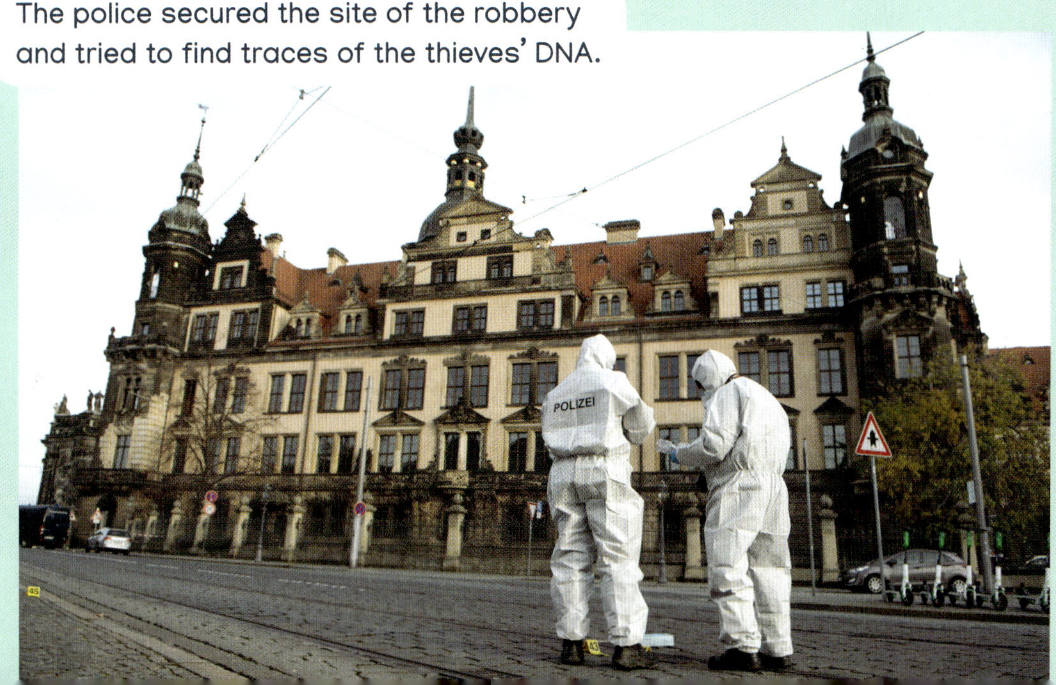

The police secured the site of the robbery and tried to find traces of the thieves' DNA.

Later that morning, many people gathered outside Dresden Castle, some in tears. They were shocked at the loss of these important historical items from the supposedly impregnable vault.

When the police checked the security camera footage showing the gang's visit from the previous day, it gave them important clues for solving the crime. The police suspected that a criminal gang, which had been responsible for other brazen robberies, had done this one, too. And they were right!

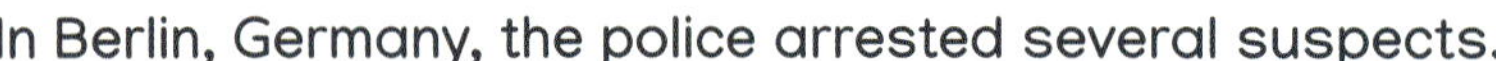

In Berlin, Germany, the police arrested several suspects.

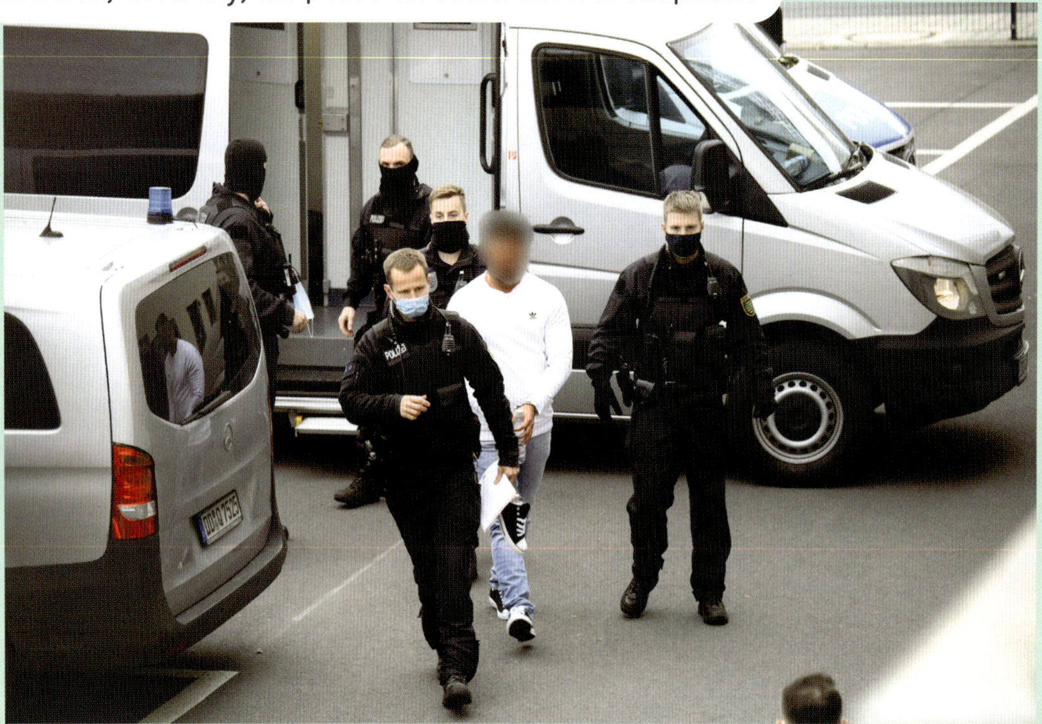

Value of the Jewels

The stolen jewels were worth about $180 million. Police believe the larger gemstones were cut into smaller sizes for quick sale. The gang might not have realised that the complete **settings** were worth much more than the individual stones within them.

In 2023, five men were sent to prison for the heist. Many of the jewels were recovered, but some had been badly damaged, including the diamond-covered hilt of the sword. It seemed that the thieves had tried to clean the jewels with a household cleaner and permanently damaged them. Some of the jewels have not been found.

Fortunately, the Dresden Green Diamond was on loan to a New York gallery at the time of the heist. It was returned to the vault, and the museum's security was upgraded!

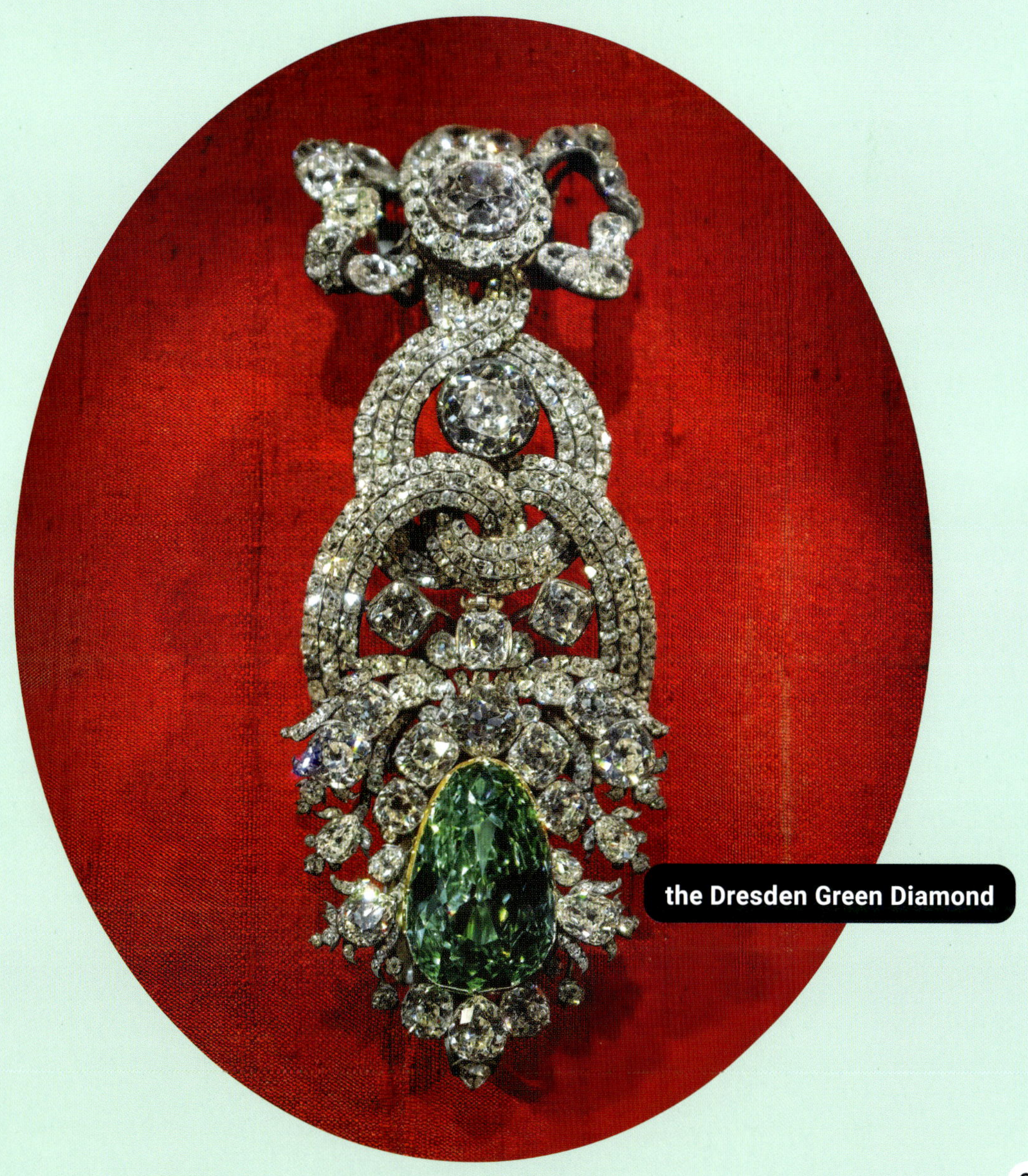

the Dresden Green Diamond

Protecting Treasured Artworks

These famous heists might read like stories from popular books and films, but it is important to remember that treasured artworks are put on display in art museums and galleries for all to see and enjoy. While some of the criminals or pranksters who carried out the heists went to prison, the actions of all of them led to improved security measures. Today, CCTV and motion detector alarms are standard equipment in art galleries. Technology will continue to become more advanced to protect valuable artworks.

Perhaps heists will even become a crime of the past!

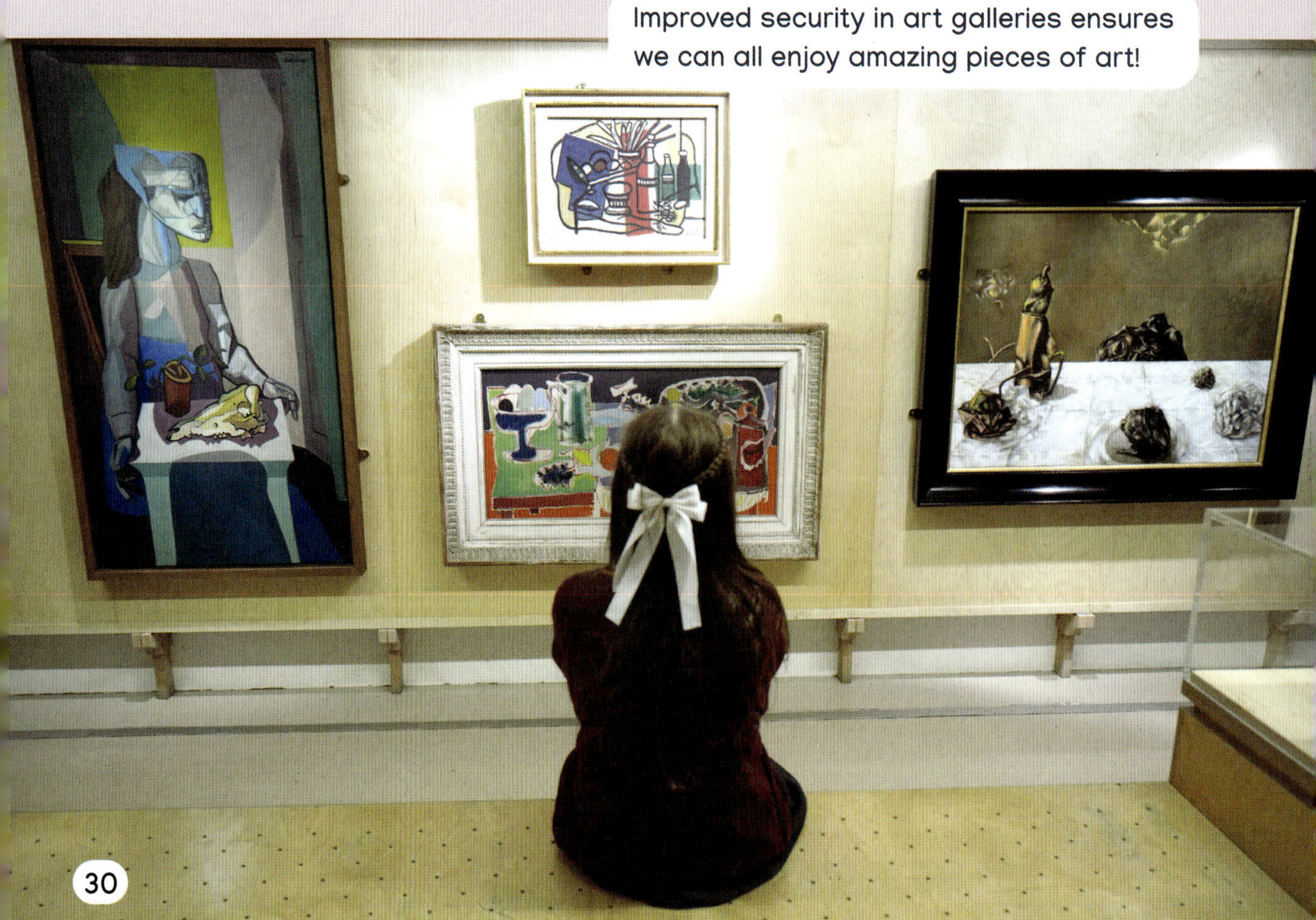

Improved security in art galleries ensures we can all enjoy amazing pieces of art!

Glossary

abstract (*adjective*)	not realistic
acquitted (*verb*)	to be cleared of an accusation or legal charge
audacious (*adjective*)	daring; very cheeky
CCTV (*noun*)	closed circuit TV; security cameras that aren't always monitored
cultural (*adjective*)	of or related to culture
descendants (*noun*)	people who are related to you and live after you
DNA (*noun*)	individual information about a person contained in their cells
enigmatic (*adjective*)	mysterious
geometric (*adjective*)	made up of lines and shapes
grille (*noun*)	a frame of wire or metal bars to protect a window from being broken into
heist (*noun*)	a robbery, especially of valuable art or jewellery
impregnable (*adjective*)	unable to be broken into
intact (*adjective*)	in its original state
masterminded (*verb*)	thought up and planned meticulously
masterpiece (*noun*)	an artwork of the highest quality
motion detectors (*noun*)	machines that sense movement
motives (*noun*)	reasons for doing something
patriotic (*adjective*)	loyal to one's country
ransom notes (*noun*)	written demands for something in return for freeing or returning items
Saxony (*noun*)	a state in the east of Germany
scoped out (*verb*)	checked something out in detail to get information
settings (*noun*)	jewellery artworks that are composed of several different pieces
subject (*noun*)	a person shown in an artwork
vault (*noun*)	a strongroom with thick walls and a door to store valuable items

Index